Confessions of a Rescue Dog

Helen Kuusela

Illustrated by Mike Kuusela

Published by Firdemonte Press
www.FirdemontePress.com
info@firdemontepress.com

Confessions of a Rescue Dog
Copyright © 2014 Helen Kuusela, MPA, MBA
All rights reserved.
No part of this publication may be reproduced, distributed or transmitted in any form or by any means, or stored in a database or retrieval system, without the prior written permission of the publisher, excepting brief quotes used in reviews.

The characters and events in this book are fictitious. Any similarity to real persons, living or dead, is coincidental and not intended by the author.

A portion of this book's sales will go to the local Humane Society shelter in the county where the author lives.

ISBN 10:061595846X
ISBN-13: 978-0615958460

For Mikayla, our little Princess
With lots of love, Farmor

CONTENTS

	Acknowledgments	i
	Prologue	Pg 1
1	Hello World	Pg 3
2	What's Up?	Pg 6
3	Goodbye Mother	Pg 8
4	The Birthday	Pg 10
5	I'm a Big Boy	Pg 13
6	Grace Arrives	Pg 16
7	I Have a Plan	Pg 18
8	The Escape	Pg 21
9	Life Is Hard	Pg 25
10	My Big Brother	Pg 27
11	Homeless	Pg 30
12	Shelter Life	Pg 34
13	My New Home	Pg 38
14	Life Reimagined	Pg 40
15	The Art of Playing	Pg 43
16	A Mystery in the Making	Pg 46
17	The Wedding	Pg 49
18	I'm Flying	Pg 52
19	Taste of Florida	Pg 56
20	Mister Magician	Pg 59

21	The Fox	Pg 62
22	Visiting Friends	Pg 64
23	Signs of Change	Pg 67
24	More Surprises	Pg 70
25	The Unknown Male	Pg 73
26	Going Shopping	Pg 75
27	Good News!	Pg 78
28	Snakes and Miracles	Pg 81
29	Goodbye North	Pg 84
30	The Big Move	Pg 87
31	An Ordinary Day	Pg 90
32	Doggy Dentures	Pg 93
33	The Storm	Pg 96
34	Our Princess	Pg 99
35	The Treasure	Pg 102
36	Mom travels to Africa	Pg 106
37	Doggy Fashions	Pg 109
38	Going Boating	Pg 112
39	Labor Day Labor	Pg 115
40	I'm a Volunteer	Pg 118
41	Halloween	Pg 121

Confessions of a Rescue Dog

42	Boxing Day	Pg 124
43	I'm a Happy Blogger	Pg 127
44	My Photo Album	Pg 130
45	Grannies and Kids	Pg 132
46	Taking Care of Fitness	Pg 135
47	Just a Little Mischief	Pg 139
48	My Solo Vacation	Pg 144
49	Inventions for Dogs	Pg 147
50	Bleached	Pg 150
51	Search and Rescue	Pg 153
52	Deputy Sheriff	Pg 157
55	Canada Next!	Pg 160
54	Hello Sam!	Pg 163
55	Hello Cats!	Pg 166
56	The Lottery	Pg 169
57	Tomorrow	Pg172

ACKNOWLEDGMENTS

Thanks Mike for your creative illustrations and encouragement along the way.

Thank you to my friend and NaNoWriMo writing buddy Jackie Phillips for your tireless cheering when I was struggling with the manuscript last November.

Thank you to my editor Robert Miller for your invaluable help in getting this book into shape, and to my friend Rhoda Blade-Charest for your great suggestions for improvements.

I also want to thank all staff and volunteers in countless animal shelters near and far for your loving care of homeless animals and your tireless efforts to find them forever homes.

Last but not least, thanks to our little poodle for being the inspiration for this book.

"Rescue animals aren't broken. They've simply experienced more life than other animals. If they were human, we would call them wise. They would be the ones with tales to tell and stories to write... animals dealt a bad hand, but who responded with courage. Don't pity a shelter animal. Adopt one! And be proud to have their greatness by your side." -Anonymous

PROLOGUE

It's almost eight on a Sunday morning and you guys are still sleeping. *Sniff, sniff.* That's a waste of time. Mom, I said good morning *to you*. Do you know what day it is? First, it's my birthday. Second, it's also the Game Day. I was expecting breakfast in bed! A *super big bowl* of birthday treats or something equally innovative. *Sniff.*

Sunday or not, you'll need to take me out now. And I mean *nowff.* Otherwise I'll be forced to go on the plush area rug in the living room. I know you don't like that option. We tried it once. That's when I learned you can raise your voice. If I raise my leg in the house, you raise your voice. Not pleasant: not for me, not for you. Let's go, get up! And put on your shorts and proper shoes. The old silk robe won't do. Today is my birthday and we'll go for a morning run in the park. I run, you walk. And when I stop to read my morning paper, you can use your iPhone. That's ok as long as you can juggle the phone and the bag.

Second, you can make your coffee when we come back. *Provided* you also give me a special breakfast while your machine is making all those noises. No-no, don't you think dry food will do, it's my birthday. You better have some savory chicken stew of the right kind: small and toy, mature adult. You'll need to change my water too, and drop a piece of cheese, please. You're so clumsy anyway, so why not today? Just a little "oh I dropped something", and I'll clean it up for you. That's a promise, even if it's a piece of ham.

After breakfast we'd better get some exercise. Don't think gym on my birthday mom, please don't! We can exercise right here at home, together is better. We'll str*eee*tch, run after my toys and jump up and down on the blue sofa in your office. You know, the one with the Mexican blanket on it. When we're done, we can make a daybed of the blanket. You can help me scratch until it feels right, and then you can take a shower. That's if you absolutely have to.

And then...I'm sure someone will call me on Skype. I know the ringtone. You can't fool me on that one. We'll both sit down at the computer and talk. I hope it'll be my friend Amelia or my cousin Pebbe. Oh, I forgot, you should upgrade your Skype to the *sniff-and-smell* version. It would be so much better for me, and I'm sure it wouldn't cost that much. Besides, you can always save somewhere else. I know! I can skip my next bath! It's an excellent savings option, no cost for shampoo. There you go.

And the game will begin around six in the evening. See, we have so much to do. A whole day of celebrations! I hope you heard that. Get up mom! I told you *I'm going nowff...*

This is what's happening today, but I should probably start my story from the beginning. It's likely to be a messy mix of love, courage and tricks. I'm happy that you will join me.

1 HELLO WORLD!

Oops! I land on something hard! It's so cold! Up to now I've been tightly tucked in a warm, cozy place with my littermates, and now I'm out of there! What happened?

I have to breathe! The air is cool, but it's so nice to breathe. I have to do it again...*aaah! Sniff, sniff.* I'm not alone. Who's there? I sniff some more. The smell is familiar somehow, it must be my mother. Oh, there is my sister to my left. *Sniff.* And my brother to my right. I can't see anything because my eyes won't open, and it's still very quiet. But I feel hungry.

There is a delicious smell of food somewhere close by. I think my sister has already found it. She's moving a little bit. Mother is offering something to eat. I found it too! The milk is warm and so good! Now I will need to sleep. Sleep and sleep. And drink more milk. Then sleep again.

Little by little I start feeling stronger. But my eyes and ears will not open yet. And I still sleep a lot, close to our mother, between my siblings. Sometimes I feel being touched by something or someone, being moved around, lifted up and put down again. But I don't know, nor do I care, much about the world outside our warm bed.

I don't know much about time either, but one morning I wake up to noises! My sister is making sucking sounds. She's a good eater! And there are some other noises that I don't recognize as well.

And suddenly my eyes start opening too. First a little light seeps in. I close them quickly. It's too bright! But then I get curious. What's out there? I have to find out. So I open my eyes little more and peek out.

Oh my! I can see shadows. Something is moving close to our bed, a huge face comes closer. Then a big hand lifts me up. Oops, high up we go. I feel lightheaded! Everything looks strange from up here. The hand is warm and my whole body fits in it. "Look, he's opening his eyes, right on his tenth day," I hear a soft voice say. I'm a bit scared. All I want is to be put back down by my mother.

Instead, more big shapes are moving closer. Lots of voices. I don't understand all of it, but the voices are excited. Put me down already! I'm hungry again, and I don't want my litter-mates to drink all the milk. But the chatter just continues. I think they cannot hear my thoughts.

Finally the hand lowers me down to my mom. And I can eat. Then I want to take a nap. But before I sleep again, I peek out. No one else is close by. It's just mother and my two siblings. All is good.

***

Humans come by many times a day. I see them giving mother something. I think it's food. She has two bowls: one for eating and one for drinking. First I think it's strange, but then I get used to it. The humans also lift us up every now and then. I've gotten used to these elevator rides now. I don't get lightheaded anymore. It's actually quite nice to be up there. I can see more. And it's all new and exciting.

One afternoon the human puts me down on our bed and suddenly I discover I have my four feet all straightened out. I don't fall on my tummy anymore. It's very wobbly, I'm swaying a bit, but I'm standing up. This is too cool!

I am getting up and standing on my four feet every day now. I'm trying to move my paws. Forward, little by little. Standing up, moving my paws, falling down again. In a few days I discover that I can move my paws without falling down every time. I can move forward, sideways and backward. I can walk! This is so exciting.

I venture out a little bit. My sister can walk too. She is such a nuisance! She cuts in front of me all the time and we both fall down. Our brother can stand, but he can't walk just yet. At least we don't have a traffic jam close to our bed on the first day of our newly discovered freedom.

The next morning I notice that my brother can walk as well. Now the three of us venture out in the little room. I'm so curious about everything. There are so many new smells and textures. I learned that the chair close to our bed is hard. I have to walk around its legs, and then find my way back to mother quickly. We are three weeks old now, I hear a human say.

Days go by exploring, eating and napping, and nights go by sleeping. I love my mother. She is warm and safe, and she has the best tasting milk. Life is good.

I feel my little tail wagging by itself, and I have a vague feeling that I'll have many adventures to look forward to.

That's how I remember my first days and weeks at my kennel with my mother and my litter-mates. It was February 2001.

2 WHAT'S UP?

Many happy days and nights later, strange things start to happen. Let me first say that mother doesn't seem to have enough milk anymore. I have to eat other food as well to fill my tummy. I have my own bowls now, one for food and one for water. The food is quite good, I can't complain. And it's a good thing the humans fill my bowl regularly because this morning mother didn't allow us to have her milk anymore. Maybe it's because I've got my first teeth now? I have a funny feeling in my gums and I think I might be getting more teeth. I wonder if they all will fit in my mouth.

Another thing that happened this morning was that we were taken out in a little box to a moving house! I could see out from the box as our humans took us out of the house where we normally live and into a much smaller house. And then the little house gave a big noise, *brrmm*, and started moving! My brother was whining a little bit, I guess he was scared. But my sister and I were observing everything. So many new things! Everything outside the little window was white, and the landscape was running past fast. It was exciting and pleasant. I loved it!

Then we were taken out from the moving house. The air was cold! I could hardly breathe. But luckily we went into another big house quickly. That house looked different from home. It had shiny tables and wooden benches. I was taken inside, and a human looked at me from all angles and did strange things. I don't have the words to describe all of it. But one thing is sure: some of it hurt!

When all of us were ready our human got a pile of papers. Then we got into the small moving house again and were back home in no time. It was good to be back home again. I wouldn't mind another trip in the moving house soon, but only if we don't go into that same big house again.

I have to tell you that I love playing with my litter-mates. We play all day long! And sometimes we compete. Who's fastest to the shoe in the corner or to the food bowl. Sometimes I win, sometimes my sister wins. Our brother is the slowest. And he's a little bit shy too. But I like him no matter what.

Many humans we haven't seen before come to see us. They pick us up and talk to us. One gave me a nice belly rub today. Another gave kisses on my head. And they all say strange things, like "ooh such a cute toy" in a high pitch voice. I don't quite know what that means. I wonder what's going on. But I have to say that while I love my mother, I also like to be cuddled by the humans who come to see us. But they are not all the same. Some feel much warmer than others. Don't ask me how, but I know if I like them or not. And if they like me.

I clearly remember this as a time when I started to realize that life would soon change drastically. Little did I know then how much change was in store for me.

3 GOODBYE MOTHER

This morning my sister left with a family of humans. I wonder when she'll be coming back. I miss her. My brother and I want to cuddle more with our mother, but it seems she doesn't like that as much as she used to. She runs away, and we go after her. Eventually she allows us to curl next to her, and everything is fine.

Soon something more alarming happens. A woman visits. She looks at me and my brother, picks us up in turn several times. Then she talks to my humans for a long time. They go away from the room for a while, and when they return the woman picks me up. She puts me into a small box and out we go into the cold air. I'm whining. I want to go back to my mother and my brother. Please take me back! *Woof, help*!

But she doesn't take me back. Instead, she puts me into the back of a moving house, much bigger than what my humans have. When it starts moving I wish I could see outside. I need to see outside to know where we're going. I want to walk back home once we stop and I get out of here. But I can't see anything! It's dark here in the back, and I noticed it was getting dark outside too. How will I know my way back home? This is very traumatizing, but there's nothing I can do. I feel so lonely.

Finally we stop. The woman takes me out from the back, but I remain in the box. In the light coming from the front door of a big house I can see a large yard. The woman doesn't talk to me, but says more to herself "let's take your crate into the laundry room for tonight." I soon find out what that means.

The woman takes me into the warm house. From the entrance way, I can see a huge room a few steps up and another room a few steps down. I see no other humans, but I can hear a little girl's voice calling for her mother from somewhere upstairs. The woman quickly walks down the stairs, opens another door and puts my crate on the floor. She opens the crate door, then goes out of the room and quickly closes the door behind her. Now I feel completely lost.

I try to examine the room, but there isn't much to find. Two big machines, a wire basket and something hanging high up on the wall. A hard cork floor and a tiny lamp stuck into the wall. Oh, I miss my own basket, my mom and my siblings, even my humans. *Woof, woof.*

The woman comes back. In a harsh voice she tells me to be quiet. *Ssshhh.* I decide that I don't like her one bit. But she brings in two small bowls. One has food, the same kind I was eating at home, and the other one has water. She leaves the bowls, turns away and closes the door.

I eat the food and drink a little. Then I try to sleep on the floor. It's so cold and hard. I decide to go back to my crate. It has a folded towel on the bottom so it's little softer. And I'm secretly hoping that if I stay in the crate, she will take me back home. But she doesn't come back. I finally fall asleep.

When I wake up I go out of the crate to take a pee on the floor. Then I go in again and try to calm down. That's when the woman comes back again. She sees the little puddle on the floor and gets upset. She grabs some papers from the top of the machine and hits me. It hurts. Then she wipes the puddle from the floor with the paper and covers the floor with more papers. I am happy when she goes away. But I feel so lonely. I'm whining quietly. This will be the longest night of my life.

Little did I know then that there would be another night in my life even longer than this one.

4 THE BIRTHDAY

Morning finally arrives. I can see light from the tiny window near the ceiling of the basement room where I slept. I drink some water and then do my business on the paper-covered floor. Soon the woman arrives. She brings fresh food and water – and a large piece of colorful paper. She also has a brush and a huge red bow with her.

She gives me the food. Then she brushes me all over. My coat is slightly curly and still short so the brushing is done in a few strokes. She cleans the soiled papers from the floor but doesn't say anything. She is friendly this morning. I could almost like her. I know I want to try.

Once ready after the cleanup, she puts me in the crate. She wraps the colorful paper all around the crate! She makes a few tiny holes in the paper so I can peek out, just a little. Everything is pinkish inside the crate. I can feel her putting something on the top and then she carries me out of the room.

I feel we are moving up the stairs. When she puts my crate down, I feel that the floor underneath is soft. I peek out and see I am now in the big room I saw yesterday. Grey carpet and a sofa with a small table. Further away I can see a larger table and many chairs. Close to the sofa many balloons are reaching toward the ceiling, and there are a few wrapped boxes on the sofa table.

Soon I hear someone running down the stairs. "Happy Birthday Elisa!" the woman says. A girl runs to my crate and starts ripping off the paper. "A red puppy!" she exclaims. "I love him! I want to call him Rocky!" The girl runs to hug the woman and then comes back and lifts me into her arms. Her lap is small and so am I. I feel good. I like her.

"It's a toy poodle," the woman says. "He is a boy, and he is only 10 weeks old. He needs to learn a lot of things", the woman continues. The girl, Elisa, holds me in her lap and then takes me up to her room. It's pink all over. She puts me on the carpet. That's when a little accident happens. But she's cool about it. "Oh, Rocky," she says, "that's nothing." She just places a book on the floor over the little wet spot in her pink carpet.

Later in the day I am the centerpiece of her party. There are candles in her birthday cake and many small girls and a few boys come to visit. Everyone is petting me and holding me.

A little later a red-nosed clown appears. All the children laugh when he whistles and makes loud noises, but I am a bit scared. I whine and Elisa takes me in her lap, but then lowers me onto the carpet under the table. She quickly gives me a big piece of her cake on a plate. The cake is so good! I lick the whole plate. It's so clean it shines! And my little tummy is so full. I fall asleep under the big table.

When I wake up the children are nowhere to be seen, but I hear noises from outside. My tummy is aching and I need to go potty. *Nowff!* So I potty right there under the table. Then I explore the big room. From there I walk to the next room on the same level. It seems to be the cooking room because it smells so good. *Sniff sniff.* I find a little yellow piece of something on the floor. It smells good and tastes even better!

That's when the woman comes into the room. She picks me up and takes me out to the front yard. "Rocky, go potty," she says and puts me down onto the icy driveway. I try to look at her to ask who's Rocky and to say that I've already done potty, but she doesn't even look at me. So I do my little business, and she takes me back into the warm house.

In the evening Elisa takes me up to her room. She gives me pieces of soft and hard candy before I go to sleep in the little bed she has for me in the corner of her room next to the huge pile of soft animals. My tummy aches a little bit, but I feel much better than last night. I'm not completely alone. I have Elisa.

That night, my second in my first house, I was quite happy. Nobody had discovered the two accidents that happened earlier in the day, and I had happily forgotten all about them. But the next day would be different.

5 I'M A BIG BOY

Following Elisa's birthday and the discovery of my accidents, I am no longer allowed to sleep in her room. I have to sleep in the kitchen where my crate now sits next to my bowls. But I can handle the stairs now, so sometimes I run upstairs to see if Elisa's door is open. If it is, she lets me come in and hides me in her bed. There we snuggle the whole night. I love sleeping curled close to her, it's warm and reminds me of my mother. But I am growing clever too. When the first light hits the bedroom window, I jump down and run downstairs to my crate.

I'm five months now and have most of my puppy vaccinations. Did I tell you that the girls in my doctor's office love me? They think I'm the cutest thing ever. I enjoy their cuddles and give them nose kisses. At home only Elisa cuddles with me. And she is at school such a long time every day, sometimes until it's dark. I wonder why she needs to learn so much. The woman never pets me and never takes me in her lap. If I go to her and want to get in her lap, she brushes me off and tells me to go to my crate. She doesn't like me very much. I think she barely tolerates me.

It took a long time before I learned there was a man in the house too. He comes home only every two weeks or so. He usually brings something to Elisa and she is always happy to see her father. I wonder why he doesn't want to stay at home. He is nicer than the woman, but when he is at home he doesn't have much time for me. He usually pets me when he comes and when he goes.

I have to tell you that I've been in training. I have to sit hours in the crate and then go out immediately and do my business. I am a fast learner. No accidents for quite a while now, and I've learned to sleep the whole night without needing to potty.

I went to school too, but only for a few hours last week. I know how to sit, stay, come and lay down. The teacher liked me. When she said "Rocky, come," I ran to her immediately. When she said "stay," I stopped in my tracks. She said I was a good student and gave me lots of treats. They were harder to chew than the candy Elisa gives me, and not so sweet. But I liked them nevertheless.

I also have to let you know that I've started to lose my baby teeth, and my real teeth are coming in one after the other. My gums itch a lot and I want to chew something all the time. In the beginning, when I didn't have my chew sticks, I used to go to the entrance hall and find a shoe to chew. I liked sneakers best. But the woman became very angry. She hit me many times with a thick newspaper.

I have become afraid of newspapers. I don't like the man who brings them into the house. The other day I tried to tell him to stop coming, but the woman caught me and told me to be quiet. She likes those papers. She reads them all day. Then she folds them and leaves them in all possible places. That way she can find one quickly if I do something she doesn't like.

I miss Elisa when she is at school and I'm alone with the woman. I have decided to grow up fast and go to school again so I can learn to become more astute with the woman. I want to know what she wants. Maybe she would like me a little bit if I knew how to be obedient. I don't know for sure, but it's worth a try.

Looking back now, I am proud of how I handled myself. I remember how much I wanted to love and be loved by everyone in my first house. I wanted to be a real family member. I yearned for attention and love, but I was only getting it from Elisa.

6 GRACE ARRIVES

I'm all grown up now, a powerful young man of nine pounds! I can jump up onto a bed, sofa or chair with no problems. I had my second birthday some time ago and life has settled into its usual amble.

I know what's expected of me. Or maybe it's better to say that I know what I'm not supposed to do: never potty inside whatever the emergency, always go far away from the table when people are eating, never come and beg in the kitchen when the woman makes food, never sleep on the white sofa when the woman is around, never touch shoes or socks. The never-never list is very long.

I have also learned to avoid the newspaper and the umbrella most of the time. If I remember the long list of what not to do, I am usually safe, but not always. Sometimes there is a new situation. I try to think how to handle it, but occasionally I get it wrong. Like the other day when the woman took me for a walk in the neighborhood. I saw a beautiful Maltese girl and just said a little *hiff*. She said hi too, but the woman didn't like it. She hit me with her umbrella. So now I never say anything to other dogs, unless I'm walking with Elisa. She doesn't mind a friendly discussion and a few nose kisses.

Now I have to tell you what happened earlier today. I got a little sister! She is a black toy poodle. They call her Grace.

She is just a puppy, probably around 10 weeks old, like I was when I came here. I already love her and know that I will need to take care of her. You know, teach her a few things quickly to make her life easier. I didn't understand why the woman would bring home another puppy when she didn't even love me, but then I overheard her talking on the phone. She said, "I bought another toy poodle today. Not so much for Elisa. She doesn't have enough time for the first one, but more as a companion to Rocky. He wants far too much attention when he's alone."

So there we have it. Grace is here to keep me away from the woman, to keep me from asking her to like me, to hold me. I'm thinking in my little head that it's both good and bad. It's good because now I have company. I can take care of Grace, and we can play together. But it's also bad because the woman really doesn't want any of us. The world is indeed a strange place. There is so much I still need to figure out.

Anyway, Grace is sweet. She comes to me all the time. Elisa loves her too and now we share her attention. I'm not jealous when she cuddles with Grace because Grace still misses her mom. Grace has gotten her own crate in the kitchen, next to mine. But the poor girl has so much to learn. The quicker the better.

The days after Grace's arrival were tough to say the least. In many ways they were similar to the days after my arrival. The woman hit her with a newspaper too and even screamed at her. But the difference for Grace was that I was there for her. She was not alone. She had a big brother.

7 I HAVE A PLAN

I have these recurring dreams. I am with Grace in this beautiful home. It's a home and not just a house. It's warm and cozy and we are happy. Elisa is there too. And we have a real mom, not just a woman of the house. And a real dad, not just a man-of-the-house. They are so loving! We spend time in their laps and get belly rubs and ear massages!

At night we sleep at the end of their huge bed. I feel safe and protective of my beautiful home. I am so happy, no stress, no fear, just this warm and fuzzy feeling of happiness.

But I always wake up in my crate in the dark kitchen. Grace is sleeping in her crate next to me. I think of the possibility of escape. Could we escape? How would I make it work? These thoughts are growing in my mind to the point that my little head hurts. I try to push them away. I do risk analysis. What happens if we are caught before we are out of the yard? What if we don't find a new home? What if someone even worse snatches us? What if we go hungry? Would Elisa come too? Grace is still not fully grown up, what if she can't manage a long walk? So many what-ifs. I try to push these thoughts away, but they always return.

So finally last night I did some research. Elisa was walking us on the neighborhood streets when she got a call on her iPhone. You know, when she talks on the phone she really doesn't pay much attention to where we are going. So I steered us in the direction of the next neighborhood. Luckily her call was long. I finally found the big white brick house where I had met the nice woman on one of my walks before Grace arrived. I'm hoping that the nice woman would take us in. She already has a large black poodle, but I'm almost sure that a big house like hers will have space for us too. And Elisa, if she wanted to come. I'm not sure about that, but somehow it doesn't bother me too much. Elisa has been so busy lately. Last week she only allowed us in her room a couple of times. Two times in the whole week!

So now I'm working on a plan. I will escape alone. I'll do it when we are in the backyard and the kitchen door is open. I will run away to search for a new home for us, and Grace will return inside. The woman won't notice right away that I'm missing. She will think I'm in the basement or something. She never checks on these things. I think it's because she doesn't really care.

Anyway, I would first walk all the way to that nice woman's house. I'd tell her that we urgently need a new home. If she doesn't want us then I'll just continue further in that neighborhood and beyond. Lots of dogs live there. I'm convinced I'll find people who will want to have us. I have to be confident, for both Grace and myself. I'd like her to grow up in a loving home. I have to give it a try as soon as a good opportunity opens up.

Thinking about this now, I realize I was quite naïve and youthful at the time, but in my heart I knew Grace and I would never be happy in the house where we lived. That was spot on.

8 THE ESCAPE

Today the woman is on her bad behavior again. It started this morning after Elisa left for school. The man-of-the-house hasn't been around for a long while, and I have noticed it always makes the woman more irritated than usual. She is walking around the house with a tall glass in her hand. She talks loud on the phone and is clearly agitated. I know that if we do anything she won't like she will be quick to hit us today. These kinds of days she just wants to be left alone.

When it's time for us to go out, she opens the door to the backyard and leaves it ajar. Grace and I run out. It's a cloudy spring day in suburban Maryland. I take Grace to the furthermost corner of the backyard to tell her all about my plan. She listens intently, but then she looks really scared. "Are you going to leave me alone here?" she asks. I tell her again that I will come back to get her as soon as I've found a good home for us. She still looks anxious, but I ask her to trust her big brother. Finally she calms down. I tell her to go back inside and go to the living room, close to the dining table, and lay down there. Stay away from the woman, but be visible if she starts looking around. I'm almost sure she won't. Not for a long time. That will give me time to get far from the house.

I watch Grace go inside, and then I start to run. I jump over the little gate in the fence. It's much lower than the fence itself. No one has ever seen me do that, but I have practiced many times. Jumped to the front yard and back again. Once Elisa almost caught me. She came out to the backyard just when I had landed back there. My legs were still shaking, but she didn't notice.

So now I'm out of the yard and on my way. I shed my collar behind the neighbor's bushes. I don't want anyone to know who I am. I don't want to be returned back to the house before I find a new home. Traveling incognito is best.

Most houses have a fence or at least some bushes along the sidewalk. I want to stay unnoticed so I run close to the bushes. I look and listen carefully for cars when I have to cross the street. I have to make sure to stay safe.

Now I'm out of our neighborhood and crossing over to the next. Some of the houses are huge and sparkling new here. They have almost no gardens because the houses are so big that they reach close to the road and close to each other too. Other houses are smaller, older, with big tree-shaded gardens. The day is turning grey now. The clouds thicken and I can feel small drizzle landing on my curly coat. I don't meet any people on the street. It's not doggy walking weather, and those who are not working in the city are probably having lunch now. All the kids are still in school. A few cars pass by, but no one notices me. Or at least no one stops. I'm lucky so far.

Finally I see the white brick house I had found earlier, the house with the big poodle. I do some careful reconnaissance in the front yard. There is no car in the driveway. Maybe the nice woman has gone to do some errands. The garage door is closed too. I continue to the backyard. They have no fence, which makes my advance easier. I see no movement inside the house. Everything is quiet. Carefully I climb the stairs leading to the back porch. I sniff around. I recognize the traces of the big poodle everywhere. *Sniff sniff.* And suddenly the poodle starts to bark inside the house. He has heard me! Or smelled me. He knows I'm out here.

I decide to retreat. I run down the stairs and to the side of the backyard where an old swing hangs from the branch of a huge maple tree. I sit down and wait. The dog inside stops barking, but after a while he starts again. That's not good! He might draw attention to me before the nice woman comes home. And I'm right! The back door of the neighboring house opens and a girl comes out. She is about Elisa's age, maybe a bit older. And of course she spots me!

The poodle inside the house continues barking. I try to look as if I belong to the house, but she knows better. The girl knows that I'm not one of the neighborhood dogs. She smiles and comes towards me. She asks if I'm homeless. I nod and she lifts me up into her lap. We go inside and she runs up the stairs and takes me into her room. She closes the door. Her room is a little bigger than Elisa's. She has a big bed, a desk with a laptop, a chair, a La-Z-Boy and a TV hanging up on the wall.

The girl is nice! She pets me and gives me belly rubs. I can sleep on her bed. A little later someone comes up the stairs and she quickly covers me with her comforter. Someone knocks on the door and then enters her room. It sounds like a big sister. She says something to the girl but it's difficult to hear from under the many layers. Then we are alone again, and the girl lifts the covers.

We cuddle in her room until it starts to get dark outside. I go to the door to show her I need to get out to do my business. She gets the hint. She takes her backpack, puts a small towel inside, and then puts me into it so that only my nose is visible. Then she goes out of the room and quietly walks down the stairs. In the darkening backyard she lets me out.

I briefly consider running to the neighboring backyard, but I decide to stay. I've found a nice house and a wonderful girl, so maybe I could stay here. Maybe Grace could come too. At least I want to stay the night in a warm bed. So I quickly do my business and the girl takes me back to her room in her backpack. No one else sees me.

At dinner time I hear someone is calling for the girl. Her name is Crystal. She hides me in her bed again and goes downstairs. I'm guessing she'll have dinner.

I enjoy the warmth of her soft bed and fall asleep. I wake up when the cover is lifted. It's Crystal. She puts a magazine on the bed and then places a small plate on it. She has brought me dinner! And it's not kibbles. It's potatoes and meatballs with a little gravy! I eat so fast that I almost choke. It's the best food I've ever tasted. Yum!

After my dinner, Crystal sits for a while at her computer while I enjoy my after-dinner nap on her bed. Later, she gets a book and comes to bed. We read for a while and then she pulls the comforter all the way up. I lie next to her and think about Grace. I hope she is okay. And I wonder if the woman has blamed her for my disappearance. You never know in that house. But I'm sure they have discovered I'm not there. I have to get Grace out of there as soon as possible. That's the last thought I have before I happily fall asleep.

That night I felt very proud of myself. I had planned and executed my escape successfully. At least that is what I was hoping before I fell asleep. But I would learn that life doesn't move in straight lines. It's much more complicated than that.

9 LIFE IS HARD

I wake up to a bright light. Someone has come to Crystal's room and pulled off the covers! Her face hovers above us, or above me, I should say. She gives a sigh. Or maybe she says "Oh, my God!" I'm not sure. I have slept so well that it takes me a while to fully wake up, but I understand that I have been discovered by an adult in the house. This might not be good.

I hear Crystal say, "Mom, I found him yesterday in our garden. He has no collar, I'm sure he's homeless. And he's so cute. Can I keep him?" The woman looks puzzled. She says that before discussing anything more they'll have to find out if I'm really homeless. They have to be sure no one is looking for me.

They take me downstairs into the kitchen and give me a good breakfast. A scrambled egg and a small piece of bacon! It's the best breakfast ever. I love eggs!

Crystal and her mother go to the downstairs office and boot up the computer. I guess they are checking announcements for missing dogs. Then Crystal's mother makes a few phone calls. I'm keeping my paws crossed that they don't find my house.

After talking on the phone, Crystal's mother comes to me. She feels gently on my neck and my back and finds the tiny bump that I've always had there under my skin. She positions her iPhone right above my upper back and presses some buttons. Then she says, "He has a microchip!" I don't know what that means. It might be bad because Crystal says ,"Oh, No! Now we can find out who his owner is, and I don't want to know. I want to keep him!" But her mother is already on the computer. Her fingers are typing. Not long after she looks up and says to me, "Little fella, we can take you home soon, I found your owner." Then she makes one more phone call.

Now I'm thinking *oh, no.* My escape was so well planned! I can't understand how she found the woman's address. I'll be taken back to the house, and I'm sure the woman will hit me again for trying to run away. Life is not fair!

So here we go. I'm in the car on my way back to the house. Elisa opens the door and takes me into her arms. Crystal looks at me with tears in her eyes. She really fell in love with me. It's so sad we couldn't stay together. The woman comes to the door and thanks Crystal's mother for bringing me back.

To my surprise, the woman doesn't hit me. She looks better today, somehow more put together, and she doesn't sport the tall glass in her hand. That's good for me. Elisa seems genuinely happy that I am back at the house. And Grace too, of course. She's jumping up and down.

That night Elisa smuggles us into her bedroom and gives us candy. We sleep on her pink carpet curled close to each other. I feel both happy and sad. Happy to be with Elisa and Grace again, but sad that we couldn't all move into Crystal's home. That would have been wonderful.

As I look back, I remember how happy I was in Crystal's home, and how bad I felt when her mother found my owner. Now I know that humans can ask doctors to plant a little computer chip under the skin of their pet so that they can be returned to the owner in case they run away. I guess that's a good thing in most cases. I was the exception that confirms the rule, as they say.

10 MY BIG BROTHER

Life has settled in its tracks again after my flunked attempt to find us a new home. Grace is all grown up now. I have always tried my best to protect her, but there have been times when I was not successful. A few weeks ago the woman was cleaning the house again with this machine that sucks up everything from the floor. I don't understand why she has to do it so often. We don't shed, but maybe Elisa and her friends bring in dirt with their shoes.

Anyway, she was doing that and I told Grace to come away from the living room. She didn't, and soon the machine came too close to her and sucked in the tip of her tail! She has a long tail, unlike mine. It hurt her so much that she cried out very loud! The woman stopped the machine and it took a while for her to free Grace's tail from its jaws. She shouted at Grace on top of that, as though she did something wrong. I never bark anymore, but then I did! I wanted the woman's attention away from Grace. The whole incident was the woman's fault, so I continued to bark until Grace came downstairs. There I consoled her and tried to get her to calm down.

Anyway, Elisa has less and less time for us. She is ten years old now, almost eleven. She is busy with her school and all the after-school activities she has. Like her ballet classes. We have seen her practicing in her room before she disappears for many hours in the evening. Once she even wanted to practice with me! She laughed when I tried to swing my leg back and forth. Ballet is not my strong suit, to say the least.

When Elisa is at home, many girls come here and they just lock themselves in her room. I think they are talking big girl secrets that Grace and I are not supposed to hear. I know they sit a lot at her computer. Sometimes Grace and I sit on the upstairs landing behind her door and we hear them giggling.

There is something else I have to tell you. Another dog arrived this morning. He is not a puppy and he is huge. Huge! He must weigh many times my nine pounds. I have seen big dogs like him in the doggy park. I think he is a Rottweiler. He's cool though. He stays mostly by himself, laying on the floor in the living room. They call him George, but I call him big brother, simply because he is so big. But he doesn't really care about us too much. He seems a bit aloof. So far so good.

The strange thing is that the woman seems to like him. She talks to him in a much softer voice than she does when she talks or screams at us, and she even goes to pet him where he lies. He doesn't move much when inside, but the woman already went for a walk with him this afternoon. They stayed away for a long time. Oh well, there is always room for another dog in this big house.

What worries me more is that Elisa doesn't seem to love us as much as she used to. Now her friends are much more important, and she takes us to her room only on the rare occasion that she is alone. Then she gives us sweets! I have grown to love the candy because it means I will have a moment with Elisa.

Grace and I have each other, of course. Otherwise life is quite boring most of the time. I enjoy the occasional car rides to the doggy park or even to the doctor's office. But recently those visits have not been that pleasant. I often have a toothache, and the doctor has been examining my mouth and doing things that hurt. I've heard him telling the woman to brush our teeth more often. She said she would, but she never does! This issue with my teeth has made me a bit fearful every time the car stops at our doctor's office. I start shivering.

Looking back at that time, I realize I should have understood something was up. But I was still quite naïve at that time.

11 HOMELESS

It's the morning of Christmas Eve 2004, a few weeks before my fourth birthday. The winter is approaching again. It's getting colder, and we have already had our first snow. Luckily it melted away. I don't like to do my business in the snow, it's too cold! Now I can see the grass, but it's still a bit icy out there.

As always, the house is nicely decorated for the holidays, warm and inviting. Lots of colorful lights hang on the walls, and the presents are waiting under the lit Christmas tree. This year it's taller than usual. The star at the top reaches up to the living room ceiling. I have to say it's beautiful, simply lovely. I feel a hint of happiness.

Usually there is a small present for Grace and me, and now probably for George too. I just hope it's not one of those hard green dental bones. I hate them. I can no longer chew them because my teeth hurt, but I would love to get a soft squeaky toy! Grace and I have almost no toys. The woman doesn't like us to litter the floors, as she says, and she doesn't like the noise the toys make when we chase them and bite them. But I'm hoping for one anyway. We could take them downstairs, or play only when the woman is not at home.

The house smells good from all the baking yesterday. Grace and I get our breakfast in the kitchen. Kibbles as usual. I was hoping for some soft food, something special because it's Christmas Eve. Then we are let out in the backyard to do our stuff. We are running around and playing to stay warm until the woman comes to let us in.

After we come in, the woman tells us that we'll go for a ride. We are happy, jumping up and down. It's difficult to contain our joy as we both love car rides, and with it being almost Christmas today, we are probably not going to the doctor's office. There is nothing better than a holiday car ride! Maybe we'll get some special treats if we're lucky.

Elisa is visiting her friend so she's not coming with us. The woman puts us in the back seat of her car where she knows we like to sit. We can see out a little bit if we stretch. This time I don't recognize the streets we're traveling. We ride for about 25 minutes, then the car stops. I try to see where we are. I can see a large building that I don't recognize. I have never been here before. I wonder if this is a shop and if we'll need to wait in the car.

The woman goes out and leaves us in the car. I must have been right, although this building doesn't look like a shop. No big windows, not many other cars parked upfront. She goes into the building. We wait.

After a while the woman comes out again, and this time she takes us in. The entry hall looks like a reception area. There is a big counter upfront, and a few chairs and small tables sprinkled around the large room. The woman writes something at the front desk and gives the attendant some papers. Then she talks to someone else who has come in from the back of the room. I overhear the woman saying, "Can't have them. They are lap dogs and want too much attention. I prefer dogs that keep to themselves." What does that mean? The attendant behind the desk looks puzzled too, like she doesn't get it either. Of course we love our family and want to be part of it, despite everything. We always try to be on our best behavior so that our family will love us back. But I know that only Elisa does, and she is not here.

Then Grace and I are taken into the back room by someone nice. She carries us under both her arms and talks softly. "Don't you worry, everything is going to be all right." I wonder if there is a reason to worry. We were supposed to go for a ride, and then get presents and good holiday food, but now we are taken somewhere in this big building. What's going on?

We come to a room that is full of small cages. Small dogs look at us curiously, and some of them greet us with a bark. The friendly attendant puts us in a larger empty cage. It has two little beds in the back and two bowls on the side. The front has some kind of bars, but you can see through them well. Our cage is clean and bright, but it's not home. Grace and I are confused now. She starts to shiver and whine. That means she is frightened. I feel the same way, but I try not to show it to her. I'm the big brother and have to remain strong for both of us. I'm sure the woman will come back soon and take us home. Or Elisa will.

We wait and wait, but no one comes back for us. Nice girls and boys come by to pet us and give us food and water. Much later in the evening we are given a long bath, and we even get some treats. They are a bit hard for me to chew, but I try my best.

It's late night now and nobody has come to take us back to the house. Now I start to fear we will never go back to the only home we have ever known. Why? I try to think hard if I had done something bad. The only thing I can imagine is that I had taken a slipper from the entry hall the day before. Just to play with it a little bit because we have no toys. Not to bite it or anything like that. But the woman didn't like it. She hit me with a newspaper. She shouted and hit Grace too. It was all so sad.

This is going to be the longest Christmas night ever. I can't sleep. I am just thinking and thinking. I start to realize we are homeless, abandoned at an animal shelter. What will happen to us now?

Looking back at it now, years later, I have to say that the Christmas night of 2004 was my longest, most traumatizing and worst night ever.

12 SHELTER LIFE

We wake up in our cage on Christmas morning. We are given food and water by a friendly girl. She pets us both and even takes us up in her lap for a little while. It's nice of her, but she is busy and needs to look after all the other dogs as well. After we finish our meals, an older woman comes to take us out for a walk.

Later in the morning we are taken out of our cage. We get a quick brush-up. Then the nice girl holds me in her lap and another girl takes pictures. The same happens with Grace.

After the photo session something special happens. The girl, they call her Amanda, touches my forehead. "You are Bumble now," she says. "That's your new name. Bumble. No more Rocky." I have to admit, I never understood why my name had to be Rocky in the first place. It sounds so hard, like a fighter, but I'm so soft! The girl tells Grace that her name will be Beatrice. Her name is so long that right off the bat I decide to call her Bea. Bumble and Bea. It feels right, and if I could taste it, I'm sure it would taste good! It might take a little while, however, to get used to these new names.

Otherwise our Christmas Day is quiet. We are well taken care of by the caring staff, but we are at a shelter, abandoned by our family. I still don't understand why, I probably never will. We sleep close to each other, and when we're awake, we listen to the other dogs talk. Some of them have been here for several days, weeks and even months. They tell us that families will be coming in again after the holiday to look at all of us. Maybe we would get a new home, maybe not. Some were lucky, others were not so. And we were not puppies any longer. Deep inside I want to be optimistic, but there is this nagging feeling of fear. Again, I try to be strong for my sister.

The next morning Amanda comes in to see us again. She brushes us and tells us that today, and for the rest of the week until the New Year, people would come and see us. She tells us that after our pictures were posted online, they had already received a few phone calls about us! She said she was hopeful that we would be adopted to good homes. This is great news! Maybe I should be carefully optimistic about life after all. But first we would be seen by a doctor. Amanda says that although our paperwork was in order, the doctor wants to examine us.

I am taken into a small examination room, similar to the one I am used to at our doctor's office. My temperature is taken, and a nurse technician listens to my heart and my breathing. She examines me all over, even looks into my ears and finally into my mouth. She looks a bit shocked and shakes her head.

Then the doctor comes in. He is an older man with almost white hair and friendly eyes. I like him immediately. He listens to my heart and my breathing again and then looks into my mouth. "Oh my, what happened here?" he says. "We need to take care of your teeth before you go anywhere." I try to tell him that I've had toothache every now and then, but I'm not sure he understands. I get one injection and then I'm taken back into the cage. Bea is already there.

In the afternoon people come to see us. Some pick me up and some others are interested in Bea. They hold us for a while and then put us back into the cage. We are on our best behavior and get lots of smiles.

At the end of the day I'm a bit disappointed. No family took us with them when they went home. But before Amanda goes for the day she comes to see us again. She explains that no family can take us home yet because they want to find the best possible homes for us. So they will allow many families to see us before the New Year and then make a decision. She also says she knows for sure now that we will get a new home, either together or separately.

In the next few days lots of people come to see us, either me or Bea. Finally New Year's Eve arrives. In the morning a woman in a red winter coat comes in. She walks right towards our cage. I'm jumping up, I want her to pick me up! And she does! She holds me carefully in her lap. She takes me out of the room where our cage is and out to a nice playing area. Then I sit in her lap for a long time. She holds me and hugs me, lifts me on her shoulder and walks around with me. She holds me like she would never let me go. I can sense her warmth and her love. I feel safe and happy.

When we come back to the play area Bea sits in the lap of another woman. All four of us stay there for another half hour and a staff member is observing us. Then the woman puts me back into the cage and leaves. I'm truly disappointed again. Why couldn't I go home with her? I miss her!

To my great surprise, the woman with the red coat comes back the day after New Year. But this time she doesn't come alone, she comes back with a man. I guess it's the man of the house. I'm so excited! They pick me up again, and we play in the other area for an hour. They tell me that they want to give me a new home! I try to tell them that I want to go home with them right now. But again I'm being returned to the cage.

More days go by and no one is coming to see me anymore. What does that mean? Did the red-coated woman and her man of the house decide they don't like me after all? Amanda tells me not to worry, but it's not so easy to stay optimistic for such a long time.

One morning I'm taken to the doctor's office again. This time I find myself falling asleep. I'm dreaming that something strange is going on in my mouth, and when I wake up I feel some pain in my gums and my teeth. The nice doctor tells me that he cleaned my teeth while I was sleeping. Wow, that was good service! My teeth were a bit sore but they felt so clean!

That evening Amanda comes to see us again. She tells us that I would have a new home soon, and Bea would too, but a different one. They just needed to do interviews and home visits. She said that they did *due diligence*, whatever that means.

That night I slept a bit better. I was hoping that my new family would come and get me soon. And if Bea and I could not go to a new home together, I hoped she would also get a wonderful home.

13 MY NEW HOME

Due diligence must be something good because a few days later the woman with the red coat came back with the man. Amanda tells me that she is my new mom and the man of the house is my new dad! Mom and dad! I would finally be going to my forever home! I see Bea's new mom is coming to get her too. We exchange nose kisses and promise to keep in touch.

My new mom carries me to a red car. I'm shivering a little bit, out of sheer excitement, but also a little bit because I have no idea where we would be going. I sit in my new dad's lap and dream about my new home. We drive for a good half hour and finally stop in the driveway of a large brick house with a big garden.

Oh my! My new home is big! I stop in the entry hall and see a kitchen right in front of me, a living room that opens to a dining room on the right and a family room to the left. I quickly decide to run around the rooms. My feet are slipping on the wood floors. *Sniff, sniff.* No other dogs have been here.

I follow the hall towards the family room and find a small room full of books. It has to be a library. And there is a door ajar next to that room. I sneak in and almost fall down the stairs! But I get the hang of it and run down the steps. Oh, here we have another big room with a fireplace, a pool table and a bathroom. I run up the steps again. This is a lot to take in.

Then I see the stairs that go upstairs. I'm so excited! I run up and see several smaller bedrooms and a bath. Finally I end up in a large bedroom. There is a silky soft light blue area rug. And there is a tiny accident! Oh my, how did that happen? I didn't want to do that! What is my new mom going to say? Is she going to think I'm not housebroken? This is too embarrassing! My tail goes between my legs. It stays hidden there. What am I supposed to do?

My new mom comes upstairs looking for me. Right away she sees the accident site. She doesn't hit me, she doesn't scream. She takes me in her lap and carries me downstairs. Then she opens the patio door in the kitchen and lets me out in the backyard. "Go potty now," she says. I still feel horrible and my tail stays between my legs. My new mom understands it means I'm so sorry. When I come back inside, I find her cleaning the accident site. She looks at me and says, "I trust you will not pee on mom's rugs anymore." And I don't want to betray her trust. It's the foundation for love, and it's precious. So I promise myself not to become so excited that I forget to go out for my business.

I find my crate and my bowls in the kitchen, but when the evening comes, I also find a little blue bed in the big bedroom upstairs. When mom and dad go to bed I follow them upstairs and go to sleep in my new bed. It's soft, and for the first time in a long while I sleep well. I dream of Bea, who also sleeps in her new home tonight. I miss her, but I believe that we will both be happy in our new homes. And I have a fairly sizable home to protect. I'm sure I'll do a good job despite the embarrassment today. Good night!

I still remember the excitement blended with some fear I felt on our way home. I wanted to trust that I would finally get a forever home where I was wanted and loved. I was ready to finally start a new, happier chapter in my life. It was a bit unreal and I had to bite myself on the paw to know I wasn't dreaming.

14 LIFE REIMAGINED

The first few days in my new home are full of new experiences. I am still somewhat serious and mistrusting. In other words, I am not my real self. But what else could I be, that's how I have become. My life this far has been full of disappointments, an abundance of fear-inducing events, and little love. So I am still a bit reserved despite my optimistic nature. Too much adversity does that to you. The good thing is that my new parents understand that. They are patient with me. They don't expect me to jump for joy and be playful when I'm not.

I have to tell you what happened this morning. I was eating my breakfast in the kitchen when mom sat down with her coffee at the kitchen table. She had the newspaper in her hand, put it on the table and opened it to a page she wanted to read. When I heard the rustle of the turning page I jumped. I stopped eating and looked at her. She immediately said "Bumble, are you afraid of newspapers? Were you hit using them?" You bet, mom, I tried to say with my eyes! Unfortunately, that happened many times. My mom understood, I think.

Another thing I have to learn to tolerate is the vacuum cleaner. Every time my mom takes it from the cleaning closet, I run for the mountains. Not literally of course, but I run into another room and away from the area she's cleaning. Then I jump up on a sofa or a bed. Something like that. I just have to get far away and up from the floor. I'm sure I'll get rid of my worst fears in time, although the noise will be hard to get used to as I have such sharp hearing. I can hear a spider jumping from his web to the floor. That's right. Maybe this vacuum breaks down in a little bit and mom buys a quieter one. That's what I'm hoping for. But it's not a big thing for me, and I hope mom doesn't mind when I run away.

Mom has also discovered that I don't like to go out for a walk when it rains. I'm sure she thinks I'm afraid of getting wet, but of course that's not the case. Not really. I simply have this bad feeling about umbrellas. They hurt more than newspapers. It will take a while for that fear to go away too, I'm sure.

But you can't imagine how many new things I'm learning! My mom takes me pretty much everywhere. I get to ride in her car almost every day, and I'm not riding in the back! You guessed it, I'm riding in the front seat and sometimes in mom's lap! Needless to say, I love it!

The other day she took me to a plaza with a lot of shops and a nice little park in the middle for me to do my business. Mom actually sat a long while on a bench there. She turned her face up towards the sun and told me she needs to get a spring tan! I'm already tanned so I continued to examine the environment. It's important to know what kind of dogs have been there, and I know with a great deal of accuracy. *Hmm*, I found traces of many dogs, including another poodle, but this one was much bigger than me, probably a standard.

Then mom walked into a huge shop and put me on her shoulder. I have never seen so many bowls! All colors and shapes, and some were completely transparent! I could see through them! I got so much attention in that shop! People came to pet me and they *awwed* and *owwed* a lot. I'm not sure what that means, exactly, because that is new to me, but I already know it's nothing bad.

We also went to Smart Pet. It's my kind of store. First because I *am* a smart pet. Second because I can run on the floor and meet other dogs, particularly interesting girls. Lots of nose kisses! Mom bought food for me from there. I think I'll need to eat it fast so that we can go back there soon.

Finally on that trip we went to Starbucks. I already know mom loves that place. She looked so happy with her coffee. It has a fancy name that I can't recall right now, like Mafioso or something similar. I got to taste some soft banana bread. Yummy! I told mom that we can come here as often as she'd like!

Anyway, life is full of things that are new to me. Everything is so exciting! Now I know what 'life is good' really means. I thought I knew it before. I thought life was good when no one was angry with me, but it's so much more!

So that's how my life with mom and dad started. I remember how I got flashbacks to my old life every time a newspaper rustled or an umbrella clicked open. I was in a state of constant excitement, learning tons of new things every day. Things that I should have learned much earlier. But better late than never. I think all this has made me mature beyond my years, but at the same time brought me back to my puppyhood – if that makes sense.

15 THE ART OF PLAYING

I have so many toys! Mom and dad buy me a new one almost every time we go out, and almost everyone who visits the house brings a toy for me. Not the A/C repair man or the plumber, of course, but mom and dad's friends. Some of the toys are in my crate in the kitchen, and others are next to my bed upstairs.

I don't play with them. I sniff them, but I don't dare to play with them. I remember the time in my old house when a little girl brought me a toy squirrel. I started chasing it and took it in my mouth. I guess I did bite it a little bit. It squeaked! The woman immediately shouted at me to be quiet. So I let the squirrel be. I thought of playing with it when the woman was gone, but then I wasn't sure when she would come back, or if the squirrel could tell her that I had chased it. So I didn't play. Bea grew up much the same way. We only played outside chasing each other.

Mom and dad have tried to play with me. They throw a little soft ball, and I guess they expect me to fetch it. But I don't. I just look at it where it stops on the floor. They look confused, but I hope they understand I'm not used to playing with anything. I'm still a little sad too. It takes a while to shake off all sadness and dare to feel happy. I've learned that happiness can be short-lived, and the happier one feels the more disappointed one becomes when the happiness is no longer there. I'm working on it though. Mom and dad make it easier for me. They show me every single day that they love me.

But I have to tell you that I *am* already *interested* in play. Or perhaps I've always been, but my ability to enjoy play was suppressed after I left my litter-mates and my real mother. See, yesterday some friends came to visit. They are dog lovers, so they came to meet me. Mom told me they have two rescue dogs at home. I haven't met them yet, but I'm curious. I feel that the shared experience of being abandoned at a shelter might help form a deep friendship.

Anyway, they brought me a little fox. It is brown-whitish, has a soft coat and a long tail. I'd love to play with it. My paws are itching. I've been sniffing at it many times, but I have not yet touched it. I'd like to pretend it runs away, and I chase it. Play. I'm tasting that word, tentatively.

The fox is on the kitchen floor near my crate. I'm looking at it. I'm a hunter, like we poodles have always been. I want the fox to run from me. It doesn't move. I go closer. It still doesn't move. I touch it carefully with my paw. It moves a tiny bit. I touch it again, a fast move, a little harder. Another fast move, and another. It's running! It's running away from the hunter. I'm going after it. No one sees me. Mom and dad are having their dinner in the family room in front of the TV. They do that sometimes when there is a program they don't want to miss.

So I continue to push the fox in front of me, one paw, another paw. It's running into the family room, but I don't even notice where we are going. I'm completely into the play now. The fox is running, and I'm going after it. Faster and faster. I catch the fox in front of the fireplace. I did it! I'm taking it into my jaws and shaking it. Shaking it, back and forth, back and forth! Oh, now I lost my grip! The fox flies up in the air, and lands right on dad's plate! Oh, my God! My dad was eating and I disturbed him. What have I done now? I know better, I need to stay far away when people are eating. Will this be the end of my happiness?

Dad starts laughing. Mom starts laughing. They laugh hard. They get tears in their eyes and they laugh more. "Look, he's finally playing!" my mom says. Then they laugh some more.

They don't need to tell me that I should be playing a bit away from the table. I'm a big boy, and I know it. From now on I'll need to see where the fox is running. Mom and dad look happy. They forgave me for the fox's uninvited visit to the dinner table. That melts my heart. I love them so much.

I take the fox to the kitchen and continue playing with it. Mom and dad continue laughing.

I will always appreciate this day when I rediscovered play. It has a special place in my memory, its own happy pigeon hole. I had been a puppy all over again, and I know that play will keep me young for the longest time.

16 A MYSTERY IN THE MAKING

Almost a year has gone by since I came home to mom and dad on that cold January day early this year. Time flies when one gets older, or is it when one is happy? My fifth birthday is only a few weeks away!

I want to tell you that it took almost a year, but I am completely back to my real self now. The self I was meant to be when I was a tiny puppy playing with my litter-mates. I'm happy, optimistic, curious, adventurous, and trusting of people. My tail is constantly wagging. Mom said the other day that my tail goes 50 miles an hour! I don't think she really measured the speed, but I agree that it goes a little bit fast. Mom also jokes that it would be a good duster. She is rough like that sometimes, but I guess we're even because I joke about her too.

It's mid-December now and my home is decorated for the holidays. I like the decorations and the good smelling tree, but they also remind me of last year when Bea and I were left at the shelter on Christmas Eve. I don't want to think about it, but sometimes it still slinks into my mind.

By the way, Bea and her new mom came to visit us last month. It was so nice to see her! She is doing really well in her new home, and she told me she has a little brother too, a brown dachshund. So good to see that she is happy as well. We exchanged thousands of nose kisses!

Anyway, the last couple of weeks have been hectic here at home. I was taken to my groomer for a nice cut and a bath yesterday. I had been there only three weeks ago, so I thought it was a bit early. But I love to be pampered so I didn't say anything. Now I'm at my fluffiest and I smell good.

Mom has also been shopping a lot more than she normally does. I gather it's been mostly for food. Both the big fridge in the kitchen and the other one in the garage are smack full of stuff. I saw her even putting some drinks in the little fridge in the basement, and the pantry is overflowing. I try not to be close by when mom opens the pantry door. Something is likely to fall down sooner or later. But why so much food? I'm not eating a lot and mom shouldn't eat more than she is eating now, otherwise she'll need to buy all new clothes. And that's not something I came up with. I heard mom say that to dad when he wanted her to have a piece of his salmon the other night.

Also, every spot in the house has been cleaned! The rugs were taken out, all the floors were cleaned and the windows too. They are shiny. I wonder if something special is going to happen, or if mom always gets this frazzled before Christmas. Yes, she seems frazzled, but her tone is never short with me. Only with dad sometimes. She wants him to help out more, or at least stay out of the way. That's what she says.

Today mom was away for a long time, and when she came back home, she had a long white plastic bag over her shoulder and several other smaller bags in her hands. She went straight upstairs to her bedroom. I ran after her to check out what was going on. Did she buy all new clothes already because she plans to eat all that food?

She opened the white bag and took out the most gorgeous dress! It was coral in color, and the most beautiful dress I've ever seen. Mom tried it on, then she put on new shoes of the same color. Oh my! She was like a queen. The dress reached almost to the floor. I was worried about her walking in those shoes. They were high at the back end, like four inch nails fastened on the soles. She was a bit wobbly when she walked. I can imagine how her feet must have felt. My paws would not have made it. I just hope mom doesn't hurt herself. It certainly looked dangerous.

And I need an explanation. Where is she ever gonna wear that dress? It looks expensive so she must be planning to wear it. But it's not for work. I have noticed she uses long trousers or shorter skirts when she goes to her office, and the dress is definitely not practical for her chores at home. I don't know if she can even bend down in that dress, it's too slim. This is a great mystery.

Even now, many years later, I remember the frenzy going on before, during and after my first Christmas at home. And I had no idea what was in the making.

17 THE WEDDING

This morning lots of people came to our house. Family from overseas, mom told me. They're all nice. Mom and dad are delighted to have them, and I am too. So many laps to sit in, and I get more belly rubs than I've gotten my whole life up to now. There is always someone to be with. I'm not able to shadow mom now so I've given up on that. I just go from lap to lap and enjoy the attention!

When the people eat lunch, they sit everywhere. The dining table is full, the kitchen table is full, and some are even eating in the family room. But poor mom doesn't seem to eat at all. Maybe the new dress was a bit tight and she wants to fit in it better? I'm not sure.

In the evening all the people go out for several hours. I try to relax and rest, but before I know they are all back at the house.

As the night progresses, I understand that these people will not go home tonight. They have packed up their large suitcases and it seems that beds have been made everywhere, in the two guest rooms and also down in the basement. In addition, a bed was made in the library, on the family room sofa and in the office. A huge strange looking balloon was pumped up in the living room. Cool, someone would sleep on a flat balloon!

Late in the evening mom's son appears. He's is not little anymore. He is tall, taller than dad, and he has big arms. He lifts mom in the air when he hugs her. *Wowf*, he's strong! Mom seems to treat him as if he was still small. It's kind of funny. It appears that he will be the one sleeping on the balloon in the living room. Luckily it's a flat one, otherwise he would probably roll down on the floor. He still might.

During the night I'm busy. Did I mention that I'm now allowed to sleep on a little red blanket at the end of mom and dad's bed? Normally it's absolutely wonderful, but this night there is too much jumping up and down. I have to go check all the rooms, do my security rounds to make sure there are no intruders and that everyone in the house is sleeping fine. Up and down the stairs all night. This is too much for one dog, I should have some help!

In the morning I'm exhausted. After several rounds of eating breakfast all the people get busy. They put on nice clothes and brush their hair. All mirrors in the house are occupied. Mom stays a long time in her bathroom. I hope she's not in trouble, so I go and check on her. She's fine, but she doesn't have time for me. No one has time for me this morning! It's like being thrown in cold water after all the pampering yesterday. No reward for all the work I did overnight.

Suddenly everyone goes out of the house. Mom is the last one out of the door and she tells me they are going to the wedding. I have no idea what that means, but I hope to find out later. She asks me to be a good boy and tells me they will be away for quite a while.

There is a shiny bus waiting for them on the street. They disappear in it, and the bus drives away. I'm left all alone in the house. I can finally rest! When I wake up, I'm hungry. Luckily mom has remembered to leave me food and water. I eat and drink, but I'm careful with the drink because I don't know when I can get out to do my business. Finally after many hours, dad runs in and lets me out of the back door. It was about time! We don't want accidents in the house. But dad disappears again as soon as I'm back in the house.

Several more hours go by. I rest. I check the house from top to bottom. I rest. I check again. Finally I hear the bus outside, and some other cars are also parking at the curb in front of the house. It's late, but all the people come into the house! More people than we had this morning, and they all talk about the wedding. I still wonder what that means.

It's a long party night! Everyone has time for me again. Everyone is happy. They are toasting and toasting. I sit in mom's lap and lick the bottom of her ice-cold glass. It has many drops of condensed water. Life is good.

And so it continues. Some of the people leave just before Christmas, but many stay for the holidays! It's so much fun. On Christmas Eve mom's son comes back to the house. This time he brings a beautiful woman, and a dog! Everyone calls them "newlyweds." I wonder if that has to do with the wedding more than a week ago. I had thought that everyone who went to the wedding would be "weds," but maybe I got it wrong. It seems that only those two are newlyweds.

They all talk about a place they call Hawaii. I think that's a place where all the newlyweds go. Lots of stories are told and pictures are shown, but I am more interested in the white Chihuahua girl. Her name is Amelia. She is gracious and refined. Her eyes are expressive. She is a little shy, with just a hint of pride, but we slowly make acquaintances. Somehow I know that she and I will see each other often in the future.

I get two new toys and Christmas cookies for dogs. Amelia gets cookies too. This is a good Christmas. I have so much to be grateful for. I'm thinking about Bea too. I'm sure she is as happy in her new home as I am in mine.

I had completely forgotten to be afraid of Christmas. This year was the best in my almost five years that far.

18 I'M FLYING

Yesterday evening something strange happened. After coming home from work, mom took me to Smart Pet again, but instead of just buying food and treats, we went to look for bags. They were on the uppermost shelf, and I had never seen them before. Mom took down two bags and asked me to jump into one of them, but I didn't feel like doing that. I have never been in a bag before so I didn't see why I should do it now. So mom lifted me into one, pushed my head down and closed the zipper around the top! It was too tight in there! I could see out from the front of the bag, and maybe I could have seen out from the back too, but I couldn't turn.

Mom took me out and placed me in the other bag. That one was bigger. I could turn, and I could almost stand in it. It had mesh windows both in the front and in the back. And the bed was soft like sheep's wool. Not bad. Was mom going to carry me in it? Anyway, we went to the cashier and mom paid for the bag.

When we came back home mom fetched two large suitcases from the basement storage. She brought them to the guest bedroom upstairs and opened them on the bed. I jumped up on the bed to check on them. They were completely empty.

Today is Saturday. Mom and dad are packing their clothes and shoes into the suitcases. Mom is even putting a plastic bag with my kibbles into her suitcase. I'm really puzzled. I don't get it!

As soon as everything is packed we go to the car with the suitcases and the little bag mom bought for me yesterday. We drive quite a while, and I love the car ride. I always do. Then I see that dad drives up into a parking house, similar to the one they have at the mall. He parks and we all get out. Mom puts me into that black bag and swings it on her shoulder. Dad takes the suitcases and we go into a big building. I'm whining a little bit in my bag, simply because I have no idea what's happening.

We stop at a big counter. The lady behind the counter takes the suitcases and then we take a big – huge – moving car. I sit in my bag in mom's lap. The ride is short and we go out again. Then we walk. Correction, mom and dad walk, I'm sitting in the bag. It swings nicely when mom walks. I could take a nap, but everything is too exciting! I have to see all the people walking around us!

And then we stand in a long line. The line moves slowly towards a man in a blue shirt. Dad shows him something and then we pass him. We go to a big machine that carries bags and then swallows them. I'm in a bag, but I don't want to be eaten by that machine! I get anxious now. Suddenly mom opens the top of my bag and takes me out! Phew! Finally, I'm free from the bag. Mom carries me through a big metal window. Yes, that's right! That window doesn't have any glass and she walks right through it. It's like a miracle! A woman pets me when we pass her. Then I see the machine spitting out our bags again. Mom's, dad's and mine, one at a time. I guess they didn't taste good after all.

Mom tries to put me back in the bag again. No, I'm not going back! At least I have to have my head out from the top, please! This time mom listens to me and doesn't completely close the top. I hang on her side again, but now I can look around properly. That's better. I see so many people walking this way and that way. I sense so many different emotions in the air.

Then we stop and sit down. Mom tells me that we are going to fly to Florida to see Amelia. Seeing Amelia again sounds nice, but I don't understand this business of flying. I know birds fly. When I get close enough, they always spread their wings and go up in the air. Where am I going to get the wings? All of it sounds strange to me. I once had a dream where I was sitting in a big metal bird and flying high up in the clouds. I remember whimpering from excitement in my sleep. But that was a dream. This is for real!

After a little while mom suddenly pushes my head down and closes the top of my bag. I am not prepared for it so down I go. Now she is putting the bag on her shoulder again and we start moving. I see a long corridor and I hear lots of noises that I don't recognize. Then we go into a big round house through a small door. Mom and dad sit down and mom puts my bag under the seat in front of her. It's really dark down here! I can hardly see her shoes next to the bag.

This is frightening, I need to get out of here! I try, but the bag remains closed. Mom talks to me and explains I have to stay in the bag while we are flying. I still don't get how on earth we'll be flying, but I have to trust mom. She gives me a few treats through a small opening at the top. That calms me down just a little bit.

Suddenly I hear a big roar and the floor starts to vibrate. I feel movement. It feels a little bit like in a car, but not quite the same. After a little while we start moving faster and the roar gets louder. The floor vibrates a lot now. I feel us moving up and up and up. My bag moves closer to mom's shoes, and this upward movement continues for quite a while. I need to get out of here! I start biting the top lining of the bag. Little black pieces of the plastic lining fall down on me, but I don't get through. I'm quite anxious now.

Soon I feel the floor level out and my bag feels better. Now mom takes my bag up and places it onto her knees. I get another treat and feel much better. I think I'm going to nap after all this excitement.

I wake up when my ears start to hurt. My bag is now back on the floor next to mom's feet. I start to whine quietly. Mom gives me a couple of hard treats. Chewing them helps my ears. Mom gives me more hard treats. Suddenly I feel a thump, and then it feels more like being in the car again. Only the noise is bad, but it doesn't last too long. Soon I feel we have stopped and mom puts my bag in her lap again. Then she walks out. She just walks and walks. I see dad walking beside her. It's so good to be out of that flying bird!

We go down some escalators and mom walks outside with me in the bag. There she takes me out of the bag again, puts on my leash, and I hurry to do my business in a small grassy area. What a relief to be free again!

That was my first experience in a big flying bird. Not quite like what I had imagined flying would be! I didn't have any idea that I would become quite an experienced traveler by time.

19 TASTE OF FLORIDA

We just landed and mom and dad's son came to pick us up at the airport. I notice that it is much warmer here than in Maryland. I wonder if there was any snow here this winter. If there was, it has melted a long time ago because it's summer-like now. The sun is shining, the grass is green and there are so many flowers. I have to say I like this!

We arrive in a gated community. I can see lots of interesting walkways, bushes and patches of grass to examine. If Amelia really lives here, we will have so much fun on this vacation! We go up to the third level. There are quite a few steps to climb, but I need the exercise. You go, Bumble!

Phew! Here we are, and we are going into Amelia's home. I'm excited and a bit nervous too. Will she remember me? Will she be friendly with me? I am always on good behavior but have decided to showcase my absolutely best attributes while here. I will be pleasant, patient and all over a good boy! In addition to my natural cuteness.

Amelia is a bit reserved. She walks around on the top of the sectional in the living room and just keeps an eye on me. She goes to her toy box and takes out a pink butterfly and starts playing with it! I'm not sure whether or not I'm supposed to join in, so I just watch. She is protective of her mom and dad too. If I jump to the sofa close to her dad, she immediately comes close by too. She climbs on his shoulders and licks him behind the ears. I get it! She wants to make sure I don't charm her parents too much. She is their only dog, used to getting all the attention. I decide to give her a little slack.

The days go by fast. Amelia and I go out to the surrounding park many times a day. We examine everything together. I'm a little faster than she is in reading the markers every morning. I tell her who's been there, and then she also goes and sniffs the traces in the grass.

We have become friendly now, but there have been a few tense moments. Last night, for example, just when I was going to sleep in the guest bedroom at the back end of mom and dad's bed, Amelia jumped up too. I remained at the end of the bed, but she went inside mom's comforter to sleep next to her legs. Can you imagine that? I'd say it was quite impudent of her to dive into my mom's bed like that. I'm sure she wanted to test my patience. Or maybe she wanted to demonstrate that I was the guest in her home. Who knows. But I didn't show that I was hurt a bit. I just generously let it go.

Another tense moment this morning was not as easy to let go. I'm a dog after all, almost human. You see, I was eating my breakfast in peace and quiet, from my own bowls I might add, when Amelia came close to me. She tried to push me away from my food bowl with her white little butt! The first time I just gave her a look, like saying "keep away from my bowl, eat your own food." But she continued to butt me. When she did that the third time I couldn't help but growl at her, and I showed my teeth! Bumble the nine pound wolf is no pushover! I may look cute and have lots of patience, but I can't tolerate being butted, repeatedly, when I'm eating my own food. Oh my, I have never shown my teeth to anyone before, or after, may I add. But it worked. She backed off immediately. After that little incident she never disturbed me when I was eating.

All in all, my first vacation in Florida was enjoyable. I love the weather and the rustle in the palm trees when it's breezy. I want to come back soon. Flying home was much easier than flying down. I had gotten a hang of it. I knew that even if it was a bit unpleasant, it was highly survivable.

I didn't know it then, but we would come back to Florida often. And I would get my own home there before too long.

20 MISTER MAGICIAN

I have to tell you that I've been away from home for the first time on non-vacation. I've been in the hospital! I got sick one morning. I had to run to do my business all the time, and it was difficult for me to make it out on time. I started feeling like I have to go soon, then I immediately felt like I have to go now, and then I felt like I should have gone a long time ago. You see my dilemma. I made lots of work for mom in a few hours that afternoon – completely without any fault of my own.

Then, to avoid embarrassment, I had to stop eating and drinking completely. That made mom worried, and I have to admit I started to get worried too. Life was not pleasant, and my tummy was really kaput. Out-of-order. I was tired, and could hardly get up on my feet.

So mom took me to the hospital the next morning. I had to stay there for two days. Two days of IV treatment and antibiotics. You know, I had to lay down with lots of wires running to and from me. I was stuck, in pain and uncomfortable, but somehow I remained calm. I'm proud of myself.

Mom says it was pancreatitis, whatever that means. But I can tell you it was a complete tummy failure, and it wasn't pleasant. First I was tired and snoozing away most of the time. Then slowly, slowly, I started to feel better. On the afternoon of the second day I felt a bit hungry and could actually think of tasting some food. I was offered a small portion of some new kind of soft food. I sniffed it carefully first, and then I ate all of it! It was not too bad. Soon I felt my strength returning little by little.

All the vet technicians were girls - and they loved me! *He is so cute,* they said. I pretended to sleep, but I heard them. They also gave me a nickname, Mister Magician!

I must admit I did a few tricks. Among other things, I got out of the IV drip and other wires completely by myself! Then I wandered around examining the place and saw some interesting things, like how they clean your teeth while you're sleeping. It looks funny with all those buzzing, noisy machines in the patient's mouth while he's dreaming away. So that's how they do it when I go for my tooth cleaning appointment. Interesting.

I think I finally succeeded in my invisibility trick because nobody stopped me. I have practiced it quite a bit at home, but mom always says she still sees me. It's been a bummer – until now. So I walked around the hospital in peace and quiet for a while before the girls discovered I was no longer in my bed. No wonder they were impressed. No other dog had managed to do that. Ever.

When mom came to take me home I couldn't help overhearing what they told her about my magical abilities. *Such a clever dog...he's a magician.* But I'm trying to remain my humble self, Humble Bumble. Nurses have to be nice to patients, boost their confidence, right?

So now I'm back at home. I'm feeling great again and have taken on all my usual chores and my exercise routines, like helping mom in the kitchen when she cooks and chasing my toy fox. I've learned that I don't have to be so afraid of doctors, nurses and hospitals. They all do their best to make you healthy again. It hurts, but it's usually the illness that hurts. Once you get rid of the illness, there is no more hurt, and you feel good again.

My dad was also in the hospital earlier this year. His heart was not functioning properly, and they helped him too. So I think even if it's bad that one has to go to the hospital, it's also good at the same time, if that makes sense.

That is still my take on doctors, nurses and hospitals. It's not pleasant when you are sick and have to go seek help, but they are usually very good at making you feel better so that you can go home again.

21 THE FOX

Today I'm proud of myself, and I think mom is too. I'm basking in my parents' undivided attention right now, eating extra treats.

You see, just about the time it starts to get dark I was out in my backyard minding my own business. I was checking for rabbit traces in the bushes near the back fence, when I discovered an unfamiliar scent. It was just a whiff of something strange lingering in the air. I sensed a hint of danger and started scanning the backyard. I couldn't see anything, not even a little chipmunk running across the terrace.

I moved toward the north end of the backyard where I could see our driveway and part of the front yard, and there he was! A red fox in my garden! He was walking under the Leyland Cypress trees that grow next to the north fence. I started barking loud, then louder! I moved a bit closer so he could see me, and I let him have it! He looked at me for a second or two and then decided he didn't want to come to my backyard after all.

That's when dad came out too. He saw me defending our land and the fox retreating. The fox was now running down the driveway and across the street into the neighbor's yard.

Dad called me in, praised me and gave me my dinner. He told the whole story of the huge fox to mom too when they had their dinner. So after I had finished my dinner, mom gave me extra treats. Lovely. I am so proud of myself. I had earned my keep.

Mom explains to me that our house is quite close to a big park where some foxes and other wildlife live. She says the fox was probably hungry and was wandering into our neighborhood to look for food. I've never seen a live fox before, but I recognized it because it looked a lot like my toy fox. I've seen other animals in our yard. Like the squirrels and the chipmunks. I chase them regularly. Or rather, I play hide and seek with them. We all like to play so why not.

I've seen a small rabbit once too. It was brown and very shy. It started running as soon as I got out on the terrace and was gone before I had reached the lawn. It ran so fast, several leaps at once. I now know rabbits don't want to play, but every morning I check if one has been in the backyard at night, and sometimes I find evidence of trespassing.

Last summer I also found a strange animal under one of the bushes next to the back fence. It was small and round. And as soon as I got close its head disappeared. That was fascinating, like real magic. I went closer and examined it. *Sniff, sniff.* The back was round, almost like half a ball, and hard. I sniffed it from top to toe and then decided to give a few little barks, just to see if it would be curious to see me and show its head. It didn't, but mom came out. She walked to the back where I was standing and we both examined the strange animal. She took me into her lap and took me inside. She told me it was a little turtle and that we should leave it alone. None of us knew how this little one had come to our backyard, but I think it's good to know what a turtle looks like.

I will always remember my encounter with the red fox. Its attempt to conquer my backyard had flopped thanks to my vigilance. I have not seen one after that incident.

22 VISITING FRIENDS

It's nice to be back home again, although it was great to be away too. I've been away for five days visiting my friends Champ and Tilman. Actually, we are not just friends, we're family now. Since the wedding.

You see, mom and dad told me they wanted to go to the beach. Not to Florida this time, but just to the closest beach, which would be Ocean City. They had booked a hotel where doggies were not allowed, so I generously agreed to stay at our in-laws house. Champ and Tilman are rescue dogs too, and I had met them on many occasions since I came home to mom and dad. I enjoyed their company, and we did well together.

So Monday morning mom drove me to their house. She told me she or dad would come pick me up on Friday. I have learned to trust mom and dad so I cheerfully said bye-bye to her.

Champ, Tilman and I rushed out to play. The backyard was a little muddy at some spots after the spring rains, so we invented a new game. We got up to speed on the grass and then went on to glide in the mud! Run, run, and *swhooom* we went. This was a sport that I had not practiced at home, so I managed to glide only a short distance. Champ won! But it was not important to win, just to participate and have fun. And we did!

After a little while their mom came to fetch us in. She was quite shocked! You need to know that Champ and Tilman are white bichons, and now their coat was all grey-brownish and mine was grey-reddish. Their mom was not really angry. Of course she told us off, but she couldn't help smiling a little too. We probably looked funny, like three muddy musketeers. Then she gave us a bath. We almost cleaned her guest bath too, shaking out lots of water before she could get a towel on us. That was fun!

At night Champ and Tilman slept in their own beds in the master bedroom. I had my bed too, but I'm now used to sleeping in a real bed so I had difficulty finding a good sleeping position on the bed mom had brought for me. It's difficult to scan the environment when you sleep at the floor level. As soon as their dad had fallen asleep, I jumped on his side of the bed. He didn't wake up. So that's what I did every night.

Then one night, I think it was the third one, I had just jumped on their parents' bed and was in the process of finding a good position when I heard something. It was such a weak sound I wasn't sure if I really heard something or not. I listened intently. There it was again. A faint rustle and it was not the wind, it was something else, just outside the house. Or was it inside? I decided that it didn't matter where exactly the sound had come from because it wasn't a sound that belonged to the house. So I barked. A slightly tentative *woof*. Then another one. That woke up their dad. I repeated the *woof* and he sat up. Now he was listening too. I'm sure he heard the rustle when it came again, because he got up and went downstairs.

I heard some more noises and then I heard their dad shout "put your hands up!" I started to run downstairs as fast as I could. Champ and Tilman were barking now too and were following me. We took two steps at a time on the stairs and landed in one big mess just in front of the open garage door in the entry hall.

Oh my! I couldn't believe my eyes! A young man in handcuffs stood in the garage. He looked scared. I would too if I had tried to break into a police officer's house. I'm sure he had wanted to steal the car. Maybe he'd seen us coming home the night before in the beautiful 1960s Camaro that Champ and Tilman's dad had just finished refurbishing. Even thinking about stealing someone's car was wrong. I growled at him a little more. He should learn that nobody should steal from anybody. Luckily I heard him before anything bad happened. A very scared and very stupid young man was taken into a police cruiser about 15 minutes later.

Now their mom had also come downstairs. I think it was a few hours after midnight. She started making some tea and gave us a few treats too. Needless to say I'm very proud of myself. When mom came to pick me up this morning, I overheard their dad telling her about the arrest I had helped him to make. He praised me as the best guard dog ever! That's a lot to take in. I have to remember who I really am. Humble Bumble. But a happy one.

This visit was really memorable! I did something I do well, I protected the home where I was staying. I was welcomed to be part of their loving family when I couldn't go to the beach with mom and dad. One needs to show thankfulness, and I'm happy I could do it.

23 SIGNS OF CHANGE

I am now 6 and a half years old. It's been a wonderful two and a half years in Maryland. I love my home, my mom and my dad. But now it seems that there is change in the air. I can smell it, and I don't like change. When things are good, I like them to stay as they are. Familiar feels safe. So I'm a little on the edge right now.

How do I smell change is coming? It's really quite simple: some new elements are clearly in play, things happen differently from the everyday routine, the stress level at home is a notch higher. That's how I know something's up. When I left my first house, I was taken by surprise, so I have honed my sensing ability. I want to know what's going on and be prepared.

I am seeing lots of shopping and packing. No big things, like furniture, but lots of small stuff. Pot and pans and other kitchen utensils, towels, bed linens and clothes. These things are not being packed in big boxes but in small ones and bags of all kinds. Some are just stacked up in different corners of the house.

This morning mom left for work, but dad remained at home. Mom left the big car for us and now dad is taking it out and parking it right outside the garage. He leaves all the doors, the lift gate and both garage doors open. That's strange, but then I understand why. He starts carrying stuff out and packing the boxes and other odd items in the back of the car.

I get more anxious. I jump into the front seat of the old Durango and anchor myself there. If we are going somewhere I don't want to be left behind! Dad tries to get me to go into the house, but I won't budge. I'm staying right here, however long it takes. I jump down a couple of times to go do my business in the backyard, but I don't go into the house to eat or drink for the whole day. I'm just sitting there. I fall asleep and dream that I'm driving a nice sports car. I'm going fast and my ears are flapping real good in the wind. Then I wake up again and realize I'm still right here in front of our garage.

Finally mom comes home. Dad tells her I've been glued to the front seat the whole time he's been packing. Mom finds me sitting right there and carries me into the house. By this time the Durango is packed. I mean completely full. The cargo space and the back bench are up to the ceiling full of stuff. Everything that had been stacked in the house is now in the car. It's incredible how much it can take, I've never seen anything like that before.

We all eat dinner and then go to sleep early. That's strange too because mom never sleeps early. She says she is a night owl. But not tonight. Change is coming.

We wake up early. It's still dark! Mom and dad get ready, they have breakfast and I have mine too. Then we all get in the car. I'm guessing it's close to daybreak. Mom has placed my black cat pillow on the backseat and that's where I am going to sleep. We drive and drive and drive. I usually like car rides, but this one is very long! We stop at rest areas every now and then to eat and do our business. I notice the air is getting warmer at each stop. It feels lovely! But the breaks are too short. I would love to explore some more and exercise my legs, but I don't want to complain. As long as I'm with my family I'm fine.

We drive the whole day! I've lost count of time, but the drive must have been much longer than 12 hours because it's dark again. It's far past dinner time when we finally stop. We arrive somewhere, but I have no idea where we are. When I get out of the car I feel a warm breeze. I run around in a big garden under some tall palm trees. I think we are in Florida! It's similar to where Amelia lives, but I smell salt in the air.

Looking at this situation with the hindsight I now have, I realize that I was sitting in the front seat of that Durango the whole day because somewhere inside a tiny seed of fear had remained. I wanted to make sure I would not be left behind. Trust takes such a long time to build up, but only one deceitful action can break it. This trip helped to build back my trust in humans: where my mom and dad went, I would go too.

24 MORE SURPRISES

Our new home is small but nice. It's not a house on the ground like we have in Maryland, it's a house on the top floor of a big building. Mom says it's a penthouse. All rooms are on the same level, no stairs to climb. It has all the furniture we need, and with all the things we brought from the house, we should be fine. I have a big backyard here too, but to get there I can't just run through the terrace door. We have to go in a small moving room for a while, and then I can run out to the yard.

I can see far from this house because it's high up, and all the windows start at the floor and reach up to the ceiling. I see lots of blue water and big birds flying just outside the window. It's cool.

I'm settling in nicely, so much to explore every day, and I occasionally meet other dogs in the gardens around the building. Most of them are friendly, and there are prospects for flourishing friendships. Mom and dad also seem to be happy. They are so relaxed! We take long walks, go on car rides, and I can even go into the outdoor restaurants so we can all go out to eat. Yesterday, for example, we went out to a Greek restaurant. I sat in mom's lap while they were having drinks and slept under the table when they were eating. After mom finished eating, I got some moussaka too. It was good!

Yesterday, mom sat me down. She does that when she wants to explain something serious to me. It's a nice habit, I feel like I'm a real family member, worth explaining things to. But what mom had to say was not fun. She explained that dad had taken an early retirement after his heart trouble last year, but that she would need to be away in our other home for work quite a bit. Dad and I would stay mostly here, and she would come as often and stay as long as she could. Dad would take good care of me, she said, and we would all be up in Maryland every now and then, and most of the summer.

Oh boy! This is not going to be easy. I'm so mom's dog. I follow her everywhere, and she cuddles with me so much. I can sit with her for hours. Dad gives me good food and takes me for walks, but he doesn't cuddle with me enough and thinks I'm like a heating element in his lap. I knew that having mom and dad both home all the time was too good to be true. And my hunch was correct, it would not happen. At least not for now.

So this morning mom left. She said she needs to go to work, and that she will be back Thursday night. I'm gonna sit in the entry hall until Thursday comes and she'll be back.

***

I've been sitting or lying here on the rug next to the double doors for a long time. Well, the whole time with the exception of potty breaks and drinking some water in the kitchen. I'm not hungry even though I haven't eaten much since the morning mom left. I see dad is worried, but I simply can't enjoy food right now. I've lost count of the days. This night I'll go and hide under dad's bed. I'm tired of lying on his little rug. I miss mom so much and now I'm no longer sure she will ever come back. I've suddenly gone from warm to cold, from happy to sad. I'm so depressed.

I'm sleeping under dad's bed now, far down next to the wall. Suddenly I'm waking up to a noise from the door. It's late and dad's already sleeping. I have to go check it out. I'm creeping out from under the bed, running through the bedroom and living room – and I see mom! She came back! She came back!

I'm jumping for joy! Mom's at home! I think I'm going crazy. I jump until I can't breathe. These pirouettes would have won me a job in the circus. Life is good again.

And so we all got used to living in two places for a while. Mom commuted back every week, and I learned to count the days until she came back. I was always waiting for her at the door. After a while she negotiated a better deal at her job. She stayed with us in Florida for four days every week and only three days and two nights back in our house up north. It was easy to live with that arrangement. For the summer dad and I also went back to Maryland. I was once again on the lookout for foxes in the backyard.

25 THE UNKNOWN MALE

It is winter, but I hardly know it since dad and I are back in Florida, and mom is back and forth again. I am used to it by now, but of course I wish that mom wouldn't need to go back so often. Or at all. She tells me she's hoping for that too. She says it's tiring to take a plane to work every week. I understand that. It must be tiring even if you do get to sit on the seat and not under it, like I do.

There is something else about her travels that bothers me a little bit. You see, I have a slight suspicion that there is another dog in mom's life when she isn't with us. I can smell it when she comes home from her trips. Someone else has been sitting in her lap!

I know it's not Amelia. Now we don't need to fly there anymore as her home is only a four hour drive away, and we always drive together to see her. Although Amelia really knows how to charm mom. When she wants treats she'll just roll over! Two times, three times, so *cute!* Oh, give me a break! With her small body, rolling over must be easy, but she always gets treats when she does that. I was briefly considering learning that trick too, but it would be plagiarism and I'm not into that. Another trick Amelia does when mom comes to visit, is to crawl the whole length of the room to show how happy she is! She whines, and it sounds almost like

"I'wweee misssssd youuu". So mom completely melts, gives her belly rubs and plays with her. I've learned to live with that though. I'm not jealous of Amelia, she's family.

I know the dog who's been in mom's lap is a male. I've tried to look through my paw on that one, but it's not that easy. Last time mom came home to us I smelled a Tibetan terrier. Although he's not really a terrier, the breed just got that name a long time ago. I've never seen one, but I tell you I'm not dreaming! I know a Tibetan terrier when I smell one. My smell database tells me he's a handsome, fairly large dog! You know, one that has a long haired double coat that almost covers his face. I wonder if he's too big to sit in mom's lap, and what tricks he performs to charm mom?

But I guess I'll never find out. I know for sure that he doesn't live in our house. There was no trace of him last summer, and mom only has his smell on some clothes every now and then. Could he be one of mom's friend's dog? I'm sure he is and that might be as well. It's good that mom has dog company when she's not here with us.

In the back of my mind I know that mom loves me a lot. She demonstrates that every day when we are together. She *walks the talk*. Perhaps being abandoned at a shelter almost four years ago has made me overly sensitive and a bit suspicious. Sometimes I still tend to see ghosts where there are none. I already feel better after getting this all out. It's fun how venting sometimes helps. I simply have to think less with my rational mind and trust more! I need to let it go and welcome the unknown handsome male into mom's life too.

Now afterwards I can tell you that the unknown male is not unknown any longer. I was right; he is a handsome Tibetan terrier with white, grey spotted long hair. His name is Tashi and he lives with mom's best friend. He's friendly. The only problem with me and him is that we are both playful, but he is so much bigger than me! It's not equal play! I have to run away most of the time.

26 GOING SHOPPING

It's mid-week again and mom is not here. It's a bit quiet, almost boring, but I have something to tell you. This past weekend was exciting! Mom took me shopping with her, and something quite remarkable happened.

First we went to Smart Pet. I found a small shopping cart, probably meant for kids. It was just my size when I stood up on my two legs. So I told mom I'd help her, not only to select stuff for me, but also to push the cart. I'm good at walking on my two legs so pushing a right sized shopping cart is no problem for me, but you should've seen the amazed expressions on people's faces. Haven't they seen anyone helping their human before? Some of the other dogs also threw long glances in our direction. I hoped that my role modeling would give them some ideas.

We bought my regular foods, kibbles and cans of chicken stew, and then we selected the treats. They happened to have dried liver. I love it so we got it. Three bags! And then mom walked into the clothes aisle. I don't understand why she always has to look at clothes! She runs a lot to the mall anyway and visits all possible clothing shops. That's fine with me because she is always in her best mood when she comes home with tons of new tops and bottoms, but why does she need to look for doggy attires? She knows that I don't like to wear clothes. I have nice curly coat, I don't *need* clothes. They are just an obstruction to swift movement. Should fast action be required.

So I demonstratively steered the shopping cart into the toy aisle. A little hint for mom. Didn't she see that the rabbit no longer has ears? And that the fox is missing both ears and most of his legs? Duh. How can I pretend they are real if they are so torn apart already? Mom finally got the hint and didn't buy any clothes for me. Instead I got a brand new little fox! That shopping trip was going well.

Then we headed to the mall. Mom said she had to get something quickly from the department store and that I could watch the car. That was fine. The weather was cool and watching the car always meant an extra treat when mom came back. Provided the car was intact.

So there I sat. First I sat in the front passenger seat where I always sit when I'm not driving, but then I started feeling a bit tired and jumped onto the backseat where I could stretch out comfortably for a short nap. But I hadn't even closed my eyes when I sensed someone was walking around the car. It was not mom because she always opens the door with a remote just before she gets in, and all the doors were firmly locked.

I stretched my head and saw a glimpse of a man who tried to look into the car from the driver's window. He didn't look into the back seat and clearly thought no one was inside. He tried both front doors and found them locked. I decided to keep quiet for the time being. I wanted to see what he intended to do. My little brain was working in high gear. This man was up to no good. What would be the best course of action in this tense situation?

The guy was still close to the car and was looking for something in his pockets. I tried to alert mom by sending strong thoughts of danger to her, but it was impossible to know whether or not my attempts to telepathy had worked. The guy tried to open the driver's side door again, but this time I could hear him putting something into the lock itself.

That's when I decided the old-fashioned alarm technology would probably work best in this situation. I jumped into the cargo area in the back so he wouldn't see me, cleared my throat and started barking using my deepest breast tones! The guy realized there was a dog in the car, and that my barking would attract attention, so he let go of the door. Just at that moment mom walked out of the mall. She saw the guy close to her car and heard me barking. She pressed the panic button on her remote. You should have heard the noise the car made!

The guy started running out of the parking lot, but the alarm had already gotten the attention of the security car that always patrolled around the mall. The guards took up the chase. After jumping out of their vehicle and running after him, they finally got the bad guy. I saw them arrest him. Mom told me they found some car thief equipment in his pockets. Apparently he was a known figure at the mall, suspected of breaking into several parked cars there. He would not be able to break into another car any time soon.

The guards alerted the police and they inspected our car. I'm sure they found his fingerprints all over the doors and windows. They also talked to mom and congratulated me for assisting in the arrest.

That was awesome. I got two treats from mom before we left the mall, and I've been reliving the excitement many times since. Mom also told the story to our neighbors in the building, and I have noticed a slight change in the other dogs' attitude. There is some added nuance of respect when they greet me in the yard.

That was a great learning experience for me. I was happy I had watched the car so well. It was my second assist in an arrest of a bad guy!

27 GOOD NEWS!

Mom has been here with us for two weeks now. She says she has vacation time, and that she will need to go back to work soon. She also took me aside this morning to explain things to me. It's always important and serious stuff, but this time there was no bad news, on the contrary. Mom told me that she will be able to start her own business in the fall, and she will not need to fly to work every week! She said she's tired of so much flying, and I understand her. I would be too, flying is much bumpier and noisier than a car ride. She said she'll be able to work from home and only fly to meet clients every now and then. That's really good news!

She also explained that we will no longer need the house up north after this coming summer. I will have one more summer up there and then we'll sell the house. Truly, I don't mind. I'm not attached to the house, any house, only to my home. And my home is where my family is.

Anyway, it's been wonderful to be able to walk *mom* again! I've noticed that it's spring in Florida now. How do I know? There's almost no humidity in the air and the winds are mild now! It's pleasant, and it's not cool in the morning anymore. Flowers are everywhere, even in the middle of the lawn. Our fence has new, bright green leaves, some of them are huge and some still small. I know this stuff – it means spring, I've seen a few. After spring comes summer and I'll go up north again. After summer comes fall. One has to be clever to observe these changes here in Florida because they are much smaller than up north. Mom says they are more subtle. I like subtle if it will get me to the fall sooner! Usually I'm not in favor of time flying fast. I want to enjoy every day properly. Feel I'm alive. I have to admit though that this time I want to reach fall quickly to have mom here all the time.

Right now the new leaves smell good and there are many low hanging flowers. I always smell them carefully. All dogs do. You know, it's like reading a guest book, Bear was here, Louise was here, and so on. I have to write my name too: Bumble was here.

Mom and I take long walks along the sidewalks. We walk as far as *mom* can make it, and then we turn. That's when I get a small treat. It's really small, like a tiny sandwich. I wish mom had bigger pockets so she could carry bigger sandwiches, but I guess a small one is better than nothing.

We always meet other dogs on our walks. There's my friend Poodles, who lives in my building. Our parents are friends so we also meet privately in our homes. His name sounds like poodle, but he is a white Cocapoo. He is wild! We run around a lot, and if we're walking together with our moms we always get our leashes tangled. They talk a lot, we run a lot, so that's bound to happen. Many times. It's so funny to see our moms going around and around, over and under our leashes, but I think exercise is good for them!

There's also this little white toy poodle girl. She has a fancy cut and always sports a pink bow on the top of her head. That sends a loud message: I'm a girl. She is beautiful too, such delicate features and friendly manners. Nowadays we know each other well and exchange many nose kisses every time we meet. I have to confess I dream about her sometimes.

Anyway, lovely that it's spring time now. The air is so easy to breathe as I'm savoring my good news.

Indeed, this time I got a good surprise. I had something to look forward to in my middle age years. I was on my fourth year with mom and dad, although it felt as if I'd been with them forever.

28 SNAKES AND MIRACLES

It's almost summer now and I'm waiting for the day we'll all fly up north again, but there is some exciting stuff I need to tell you. You see, last week dad and I took a long walk to a park that is about two thousand steps away from home. I love going to that particular park because I love to play tennis. That's right! There are two tennis courts, and people must be a bit lazy because most of the time there is nobody playing. I love to play there with a nice brown Labrador retriever, Brownie. He is a bit older than me, but he runs well. Our dads sit on the bench at the side of the court and throw a tennis ball to us, and we run after it. The one who's faster and brings the ball back gets a treat! It's fun and we run like crazy! I know that too many treats could be fattening, but since we jump up and run so hard, I think fat can't stick to us. We are both slim. These are real play dates!

Anyway, when dad and I reached the park, we walked on the small path towards the tennis courts. I was sniffing in the bushes, like I always do. I had to make sure to do my business before Brownie and I would start playing. Suddenly I saw movement in the grass behind the shrubbery. Something almost black. It was round and long. It had no legs, and it wiggled its whole body to crawl forward. I had never seen anything like that. It stopped and looked at me with its small, nasty-looking eyes! I got cold shivers. I gave him a low growl, my most scary, and ran back to dad. He went closer to the bush and looked around. Then he quickly came back to me and we walked fast away from there. He told me it was a snake. They can be dangerous, he said, some of them bite! I didn't see the teeth, but I'm sure he would have shown them to me if I had stayed. Dad said I should always run away if I see anything like it again. He said that its bite might kill me. So I guess it was a close call, as mom says. I still like to go to that park, but now I know to be more careful when I sniff around the bushes.

Then yesterday two things happened. First, in the morning when I was having my breakfast in the kitchen and dad was having his coffee, a huge bird landed on the railing at our terrace. I mean huge! Its wings were long; it had a big head, piercing eyes and very sharp claws. When he sat there, his claws firmly around the railing, I felt fear. He looked right at me from behind the floor-to-ceiling window. He bent his head and looked at me like I was a hearty meal. Me!

Dad said the bird was an eagle. He didn't do anything to get it to leave. I guess dad had confidence in the hurricane proof windows, but then he wasn't the meal the eagle was waiting for. I had lost my appetite and jumped into dad's lap. I felt fairly safe there. Dad was at least much bigger than the bird. Finally the big bird realized it couldn't have me for his next meal. He turned, spread his huge wings and flew away. Dad told me afterwards that we had to keep an eye on the skies when we were outdoors, and I understood why that was necessary.

As if that would not have been enough excitement for one day, we had a fierce thunderstorm in the afternoon. Unlike many other dogs, I'm not afraid of thunder. Amelia, for example, wants to go under the covers in her mom and dad's bed, and I know that Tashi, the Tibetan terrier, becomes anxious and starts to whine when it thunders. So it was not the thunder itself that was unpleasant. It was the wind. It shook and rattled the large glass doors and made me nervous.

On the top of the fierce wind, dad saw a huge whirling funnel of water on the ocean, quite close to our building on the beach. I sensed he too was tense. He held me and we watched how the funnel grew higher and headed closer to the beach. Suddenly it turned, and then traveled further away onto the vast ocean. It was like a miracle! Like an invisible hand had stopped it in its tracks.

Dad said a water spout was like a tornado. Luckily it turned away from us, but I was hoping that there would be no boats in its way. That would not be good.

Lots to take in for one day. That night I didn't sleep on my blanket at the end of the bed, I slept curled close to dad's side with my head on mom's pillow. Dad didn't say anything.

In retrospect, I learned a lot on that day, for example, that I need to be on the lookout for dangers that might lurk in the bushes or in the skies. But I should not overdo it. Life is too short to worry all the time.

29 GOODBYE NORTH

So now I'm in Maryland again! It's nice to run around and check the garden every day. I find mostly squirrels and chipmunks, but I smell an occasional rabbit and deer too. I have not actually seen a rabbit this summer so far, but one night mom lifted me up to the window to see a deer in our yard. I had followed mom to the bathroom, like I sometimes do, and she was standing at the window watching the deer eat her flowers.

The next day mom bought a plastic bottle of brown water. I saw her go out and spray the water on the flowers. Later in the day I went out in the yard and thought I would check the damage in the flower bed, but when I came close to the flowers, I didn't like what I smelled! The whole flower bed smelled awful, like a bunch of rotten eggs had been smashed there. So it wasn't brown water after all, but something much stronger. I thought the poor deer wouldn't want to go anywhere near that smell. That would be good for mom's flowers, right?

But I see squirrels almost every day. Sometimes they want to challenge my hunting abilities by running across the long backyard lawn, and off we go, running like crazy! So one day I was chasing a squirrel when he decided to tease me. He jumped up on the chain-link fence and then down into the neighbor's yard. That's when I saw something strange. There was a man on their patio. I had never seen him before. He was not the father or the son of the house, or the gas man. I know them all. This man was looking through the windows into the new sunroom our neighbor had built only last summer. He was trying the back door. Of course it was locked, our neighbors had gone on vacation.

This was not right. It was my neighbor's house, and a stranger was trying to get in there! I started growling. You know the scary growl that starts deep in my breast and comes out of the mouth between my teeth. Then I started barking. I never bark other than when I do my protection duties, but I know how to be loud when needed. The man looked at me. He put his finger on his lips and said *"Sshhh."* I turned my volume up a notch! I smelled fear! That's right. He was not supposed to be there, and now he was afraid of me. My barking had caught dad's attention and he came out on the terrace. Dad saw the man, and the man must have seen him too because he immediately started running towards the street and then away from the house.

Dad called the police who came out to check our neighbor's house. There was no sign of a break-in, thanks to me! The policemen were friendly and I basked in their attention. I had done something good and had the squirrel to thank for my fame. I felt warm and good inside. Humble Bumble.

After that incident I made it a habit to check the neighbor's house every time I go outside, but it's been quiet ever since.

This summer we've had many garden parties on the terrace. I like them a lot. The grill is always going, and I get pieces of meat and delicious sausages dressed as fake hot dogs. Not to talk about countless belly rubs!

At one of these occasions, Bea came to visit us! I loved seeing her so happy. We played in the backyard and had an opportunity to catch up on everything. When we got tired, I invited her to my large bed in the living room. I rarely use it anymore, but now it came to good use. It accommodated both of us for a nice afternoon nap. When they left we promised to Skype each other.

So this is the last summer in the house. It's going to be sold after mom quits her job in the fall. It means I'll have my mom with me much more then. I have told her that she can give my bed and my toys to the shelter where Bea and I spent one memorable Christmas. I already have all I need. But I think I'll miss this house a little bit, just because coming here from the shelter gave me the best home ever!

I still remember that house with a grateful mind. That was the house where I became the Bumble I was meant to be. I got rid of my distrust of humans and my fear of abandonment. And I'm proud of myself because I was always able to protect it from foxes and other intruders.

30 THE BIG MOVE

So today is the big day! My family is officially moving from Maryland to Florida. I mean we are already here, even mom arrived yesterday, but all of our stuff from the house will arrive on a big truck today. Mom and dad bought a new home a few weeks ago, just two miles from this place! I have not been there yet, but mom told me last night that I'll have a nice garden to play in. That's cool. She has definitely raised my expectations.

Right now I'm waiting in our old place. Mom and dad are in the new place taking care of the truck load, I think. Waiting is boring. I have nothing to do. I already ate all my food so now I'm just napping, and between the naps I'm reflecting on life. I've become a thinker. I guess that's because I've seen so much and all of it needs to be processed. I've seen the bad and the good, experienced pain and joy in my short eight years so far. I have been miserable but never hopeless. Somehow I always knew that things would turn out the way they were supposed to. And indeed, they have. I'm such a happy dog, and I'm grateful for my life every day. Sometimes I feel like I need to find a way to give back, help others in some fashion. I want to have a mission in life. I'm thinking a lot along these lines nowadays. I'm a rescue dog, and that comes with some responsibility.

Oh, mom is coming to get me now. I'm going to my new home! She is taking my bowls, my food and my blanket. I guess she will get the rest of the stuff from here later.

It's not a long drive, three minutes tops. I could have walked here! The garden is nice, gives me a good first impression - lots of trees and bushes, all forms and shapes. I'm sure I'll find many squirrels here. It promises to be a lot of fun!

When we walk in, I see that our living and dining room furniture is already in place, and our big bed is in the bedroom. I recognize all the furniture, but there are so many boxes in the other rooms! Brown big ones, white small ones. They are everywhere, stacked on the top of each other. One of the small bedrooms is so full of boxes that I cannot even go in and turn around.

Mom puts my bowls in the kitchen. I get my own little corner there as my dining room, and I get good food. My mom mixes kibbles with soft chicken stew. That's so good, real pieces of chicken and vegetables. Tonight I'm really enjoying my dinner, grateful for everything. I'm invigorated by our new home and my meditations earlier today.

Mom and dad seem exhausted. They want to go to bed directly after dinner. I guess they've worked hard today and will need to do so tomorrow too if they are going to take out all our stuff from the boxes. I'm going to help mom of course, so she doesn't get this tired. My blanket is now on the bed, so I jump up also. I notice that the TVs are not working. Nothing to watch before I sleep, but I'll make them all work tomorrow. I know how to turn them on once the remotes have been found. I've turned on the bedroom TV accidentally a few times. They have such good programming in the middle of the night.

And so I go to sleep. We all do.

When I look back now, I realize that the first night in our new home was yet another turning point for the better. I now had mom here most of the time, had a wonderful nature reserve close by to explore for long walks, and a doggy park to visit if I wanted company. Also, I could warm my middle-aged bones in the sun on the terrace whenever I wanted to.

31 AN ORDINARY DAY

So we managed to get through yet another day. Oh, I didn't mean to sound negative. It was not too bad for a Monday, just an ordinary day in our new home, where life has settled into its own pleasant trot. No hitches whatsoever.

But now I'm starting to get worried. It's almost nine o'clock and my bed is not ready. *Sniff.* I jumped up on the bed and checked - *it's* not there! Where is my red blanket, *mom?* You know the woolen Ralph Lauren, made in China? Did you wash it? Forget it in the washer?

I'll need to call it a day soon. Dad's already in the bathroom, but what are you still doing mom? This gives me a slight suspicion that my wellbeing might be of a lesser priority, and we don't want that. Our relationship is built on trust! You better bring my blanket *nowff.* Or are you still sour about the little *incident* today? Mom, you need to let it go!

I've gotten into the habit of reflecting back on the day before I fall asleep. It's useful. I can learn from my obvious mistakes. Like earlier today when mom left for her meetings. I should've seen it coming. "It will only take a little while, dear," mom said. I thought she was talking about mixing something delicious for me to eat because it's Monday, but her tone wasn't quite right. I sensed some guilt in it, and she spent too much time in the bathroom. At least 15 minutes. I sat behind the door. And then *puff*, she was out of the house. I should've been ready. You know I love car rides...the flapping of my ears in the wind. There's nothing more enjoyable, apart from a good belly rub, and I could've watched her car.

But she just went. And she left the radio on, not the TV. I can't stand classic rock, but I love watching dog shows and sometimes even the news on CNN.

How could she forget? Or did she just not c*are*? I can't see the TV remote anywhere. Now, what am I supposed to do? Nothing to *do* is so boring. Then I discovered she had also forgotten to close her office door. Maybe she is just getting up to a mature age, like they say on the doggy food packages "for mature adults?" That would explain it.

Her office door was open. Maybe I could watch videos on YouTube if mom also forgot to shut down her laptop. I was just about to jump onto her office chair when a faint scent reached my nose. *Sniff, sniff* – it *was* ham, positive! There it was, a piece of mom's ham sandwich from this morning in the little wastebasket under the office table. It was well wrapped in layers of soft napkin so I had to work hard to get at it, but it was worth it! There were some other interesting things too, but nothing else that was edible. I checked.

The rest of the afternoon I was pretty much occupied. I tried to clean up a bit in mom's office, brought a few things into the kitchen close to the large garbage bin, the one with a lid. I thought mom would appreciate my effort. Then I probably dozed off a little before she finally came home.

I got a treat and a belly rub. Lovely to have her home! Then she walked into the kitchen. I heard a high-pitched "what have you done here?" She should have seen what I'd done, I'd been cleaning! No thanks for my effort – she just walked right into her office. More noises. *I can't hear you now…I'm under the bed.* I started feeling guilty, but should I? I didn't leave the sandwich to rot in the waste basket, and I didn't forget to close the door. She did. Something's not right. Or fair? Eventually she will realize that. I know my mom, she'll get over it.

And she did. Love conquers all. Peace settled back into the house. Back rubs, belly rubs, a good dinner, a nice walk, more treats and a nice film sitting in her lap. Can one ask for more on a Monday?

Oh, I was in my thoughts, thanks mom for the blanket! I knew you'd bring it! It smells good. Here you go, a good night kiss. *Lick, lick.* I love you too mom.

That's pretty much how my ordinary day goes, a little mischief and a lot of love.

32 DOGGY DENTURES

Mom is talking on the phone again. I can see her walking back and forth. That means it's gonna take a while...so I'm going to sit in her office chair and borrow her laptop. You see, I have learned to use the laptop after sitting countless hours in mom's lap while she's working. I sneak into mom's office whenever I can, and I go on the net to read. How do you think I could otherwise keep up on what's going on? I write too, of course, but today I will need to do some urgent research.

You see, I'm a bit worried about my *teeff*. Last week when I was in dental cleaning at my doctor's, I got the surprise of my life. No, I didn't win a prize or anything like that, I lost two teeth while I was sleeping. Two *front* teeth!

I heard the doctor tell mom that my teeth are not good. I know better than anybody why they are in such bad shape. It's all the candy Elisa kept giving me. I should've just turned my head away when she offered me a Lifesaver or a Gummy Bear. But who can do that? The candy tasted so good and I needed to have something good in my life. I hope you understand. I didn't have the character to resist.

To make things even worse, no one brushed my teeth in my first home. The first time I saw a tooth brush was at the shelter! Can you imagine that? I still don't like when mom brushes my teeth. I wish I had gotten used to it when I was small. That would have been so much better! But here I am, with bad teeth and now two are missing in the front.

I think I will need to get dentures. I'm googling "doggy dentures," but I can't find anything, only lots of food ads! I found one site that puts dentures on my picture, but they're not real, of course. Isn't it surprising that there is something that has not yet been invented? *Oh well*, I may have to accept the new situation. Accept and then adapt. I'll have to learn a more subtle smile, and be more charming in general. That shouldn't be too difficult.

Oh, now mom is coming in. *Hi mom*, you look worried! What's wrong? I hope it's not me. I would never make you worry, you know that, and I can manage without my two teeth, see I can even smile! Just don't give me too much hard food now that my ability to chew has been reduced. Soft chicken stew is better, much preferable to kibbles.

Now, cheer up mom, let's *do* something! If you need to go to the pharmacy to fetch your meds, I'll come with you. It would be a nice drive, some quality time together. And you know I love the drive-through. I can climb in your lap and say hi to the girls through the open window. *Hi girls! I'm doing fine! You look good too!* Sometimes we chat there forever, until someone honks behind you, remember mom? Then I ask you "Shall I bark or shall we go?" You know the drill.

But mom shakes her head. We're not going to the pharmacy this afternoon. Now I'll need to plan something else that will energize mom. It's a pity that they don't allow me at the gym yet. I'm still working on it. So whatever we do together, it has to be here at home. Maybe Pilates? Stretching is good for circulation, and for mom's mood. My mood is always fine, but I can sympathize with her.

I always love working with mom. Whether it's exercising or watering flowers, mom does the inside and I do the outside. Or making dinner. That's my favorite chore. I keep the kitchen floor clean while mom is cooking.

I always look forward to dinner time, and the evening stroll. Last night I met a new girl. She's also a toy poodle, but she's black and tiny. She had lots of style, and a nice perfume. I hope to see her again tonight. You know, just for a chit-chat, and a shy smile. I hope she doesn't notice my missing teeth. I truly have to consider inventing doggy dentures, won't I?

At that time I was self-conscious of my two missing front teeth, but now I have completely adapted to smile without them. I have not embarked on the invention just yet, but I'm giving an excellent hint here to an inventor. If you start right about now, you're likely to beat me to it.

33 THE STORM

Today I have to report some new developments. Things don't seem to be quite normal around here. I mean this morning was completely fine. Mom and I had a nice Sunday stroll in the park. I had lots of time to *read* my morning paper around the bushes because mom was so occupied with her camera. There were some big white birds in the marsh. I didn't care about them; they were too far out for me to swim to them. So I focused on my favorite exercise, squirrel waiting. He was sitting high up in a palm tree looking down, and I was waiting under the tree looking up.

This afternoon things started to change. I think someone might be coming to visit. Mom went to the grocery store today! Why? It's Sunday, and she just went to the store yesterday. When she came back I saw she had bought some cans. More c*hicken stew?* But she didn't put them where *my* food is. Yes, I know where my food is, I'm always checking out the stash of treats, but mom doesn't know that I know. Which is good because otherwise she might move them on a higher shelf where I can't see them.

All these cans went into the other pantry. That's weird. The labels looked good. I'm such a slow reader, but I thought it said *ravioliff.* I am not sure what that means, but I told mom

I'd volunteer to test the food. I saw peanuts too, but I can't have them. I don't want to get sick.

She also bought a few large water bottles! Why can't we all drink water from the tap filter, like we always do? That beats me, but maybe all that is for someone else?

Then more weird things happened. I was sitting comfortably in a lounger on the terrace warming myself and enjoying my Sunday when mom suddenly came out with dad. They didn't sit down. Instead they asked me to go in. First I thought it was because it was hot, but then they started to move the stuff inside. All of it! Where do I sit now? I'll have to regain my access to the living room leather sofa. *Mom can you put my black cat pillow on the sofa, pleaff!*

I just looked into the laundry room. It's so full of chairs from the terrace that mom can't even use the washing machine. What if my red wool blanket gets dirty? What if there's an accident? Not that I have accidents, but maybe mom spills her coffee on it? She is so clumsy at times. The whole thing is puzzling to me. I heard mom talking about someone called Debby. I don't know her, and I think I won't like her. She hasn't been here before, and I hope she doesn't come now. I might bark if she knocks on the door, and I'll definitely growl.

Oh, now the sky is getting dark! I mean, not the usual dark, but a very scary dark. It's not evening yet, but all the lights are on. It's thundering too, and raining. The wind has strengthened, I notice that the palm trees are bending sideways. Then the rain starts to hit the glass doors. I have never seen that in our new home because the terrace roof is so wide, but now the rain comes sideways. Sheets of water are moving in the air. It looks like a big, pulsating shower. I'm not afraid of thunder, and the wind doesn't rattle the glass doors like it used to do in our previous home. I listen for rattle, but I don't hear any! This is so cool.

Mom is making dinner early today. She said she'll do it just in case tropical storm Debby makes the power go out. So that's who Debby is. It's the name of the storm! Mom says nothing functions if the power goes out. Nothing! Not even their toilet? That's amazing. How can the power have so much power? It makes people and dogs completely dependent on it not going away.

Anyway, we have dinner, and the lights flicker a couple of times, but the power doesn't go out. It stays inside. After dinner I have to go out. Whatever the weather, I just have to go. Mom understands. She takes the IKEA umbrella. It's the biggest umbrella we have. I just hope mom and dad assembled it correctly so it doesn't fall apart in the storm. Mom knows I'm still a bit apprehensive about umbrellas after the close contact with them in my first house.

But out we go. Mom looks like a soldier when she positions the umbrella sideways against the wind when we reach the garage doors. The wind is really howling out there. I have to do my business fast, and in we run again. I wish we had a doggy toilet inside, but maybe that's a secondary need because we don't have too many stormy days here in Florida.

The evening goes fast. We have power. We watch TV and then we go to sleep. I can hear the storm, but I'm happy to note that our glass doors are keeping it outside. They don't rattle or even move in the wind. Mom tells me they will withstand even a strong hurricane. That's comforting to know. I dream about a nice day on the beach. No wind, lots of sunshine and calm, clear waters.

This storm ended well for us. Just a little flooding on the beach and in the park where mom and I usually walk. Nothing really bad happened, and after three days Debby was completely out of here. I don't look forward to more storm excitement than what we had with Debby. After her visit we've had an "almost visit" by Isaac, but it was a milder storm. So far so good. I'm keeping my paws crossed.

34 OUR PRINCESS

I need to tell you something important. Mom has a daughter. No, not like that. She actually has a son, who has a new little girl. Mom calls her granddaughter and sometimes grandbaby. That's funny, and I don't get it. Grand means big or large, and the baby girl is small! Anyway, they don't live here so I see her only when they fly in every now and then. The first time I saw her she was tiny, but her eyes were already open. I guess human babies are born with their eyes already open. I mean when they don't sleep. She was sweet. When she slept in her baby crib that mom had bought just for her visits, I jumped on one of our high bar stools so I could see her sleeping. Lovely.

Next time they came to visit she had grown a lot, and she could almost walk! Mom had borrowed a strange, small "walker" for her. She sat there, and she could walk back and forth with it. I didn't have anything like that when I was learning to walk, but it seemed practical.

Mom goes to see her every now and then. Every time she comes home, she tells me the baby has grown more. I was all grown up when I was about 18 months old, but I guess human babies grow much slower. I wonder how tall she's gonna be when she is all grown up?

Last Christmas we all went to see her. I could go too because they had moved back to Florida. It was a nice drive for about four hours! We had a short break in the middle so we all could go and do our business, but the journey went fast. I so looked forward to seeing Amelia again!

Amelia greeted me right at the door! She was still beautiful, not aged at all. She was much calmer now, kind of more grown up. I hoped we wouldn't need to do the growl and the wolf look this time around. Of course she still played up to mom by crawling the whole length of the living room towards her and then rolling around expecting treats! But that was okay I guess.

The baby had grown even more now. She was two years old and could run around in her little blinking shoes. I had forgotten how much I love little kids! She liked me a lot too! You know, between all the running and playing, she wanted us to sit together in her dad's old La-Z-Boy! We would sit there, and she would put her little arm around my neck. We would just sit there and snuggle. She would hug me and I would protect her.

Then she would cook me some tea in her little kitchen and give me tiny biscuits. I had to pretend to drink the tea, but the biscuits were real, like tiny stars. Or they may actually have been her cereal stars, I'm not sure. That was a fun tea party. Then we would tricycle around her playroom. She was pedaling and I was sitting on the cargo tray in the back! We had such a good time!

On Christmas morning she would get lots of presents! She would open them fast and even help others to open their presents. I got a little squirrel from her. Her favorite present was the bubble machine! It was like a small carriage she could push ahead of her, and it would spit out huge bubbles. Then we would both run after them. I guess the little Princess and I formed a special bond from the time she was big enough to understand I was a dog, an especially patient dog.

So every time we have seen each other since Christmas we have been sitting and cuddling in an easy chair. Last time she came here, we were even allowed to climb up in mom's best leather chair, and sit there close to each other. That was lovely. I miss her all the time when she's not here. It's lovely to have a little Princess in our family!

Now our Princess has grown even more, she'll have her fourth birthday in a few months! We still play a lot, sit and cuddle, and she talks to me on Skype all the time!

35 THE TREASURE

Now I have to tell you something exciting, or more accurately, something significant. One day last week, mom and I were walking in the nearby nature reserve. As usual, she was taking pictures with her camera, and I was going about my business. There is a nice picnic area in the middle of the park surrounded by old trees. I like to sniff around that area because other families also bring their dogs there. I can always find new, exciting smells. So after snapping a few pictures of the trees, mom was sitting down on one of the wooden benches so I could roam around and examine the area.

Anyway, midway into my tour of the picnic place I was sniffing under a set of two old-looking swings, when I traced a smell that merited some further research. So I started digging. And digging more. There was a small, old bone buried in the sandy soil! It was fairly small and completely white. Mom saw it and ran to take it away from me. She said I should not be eating anything I found in the ground. I could get sick, and we would have to go to the hospital again. I didn't like that idea so I let her have the bone, reluctantly. She went and threw it away in a large waste bin. All that work for nothing! But I had unknowingly unearthed something else as well. When mom came back to the swings, she bent down and picked up something shiny that was still partially in the ground. It looked like a golden ring, and there was a big, bright stone planted on it too!

Mom was delighted by my find. This time she did not go and throw it away, but took a napkin or something from her pocket and cleaned it up a bit. Then she put it in her pocket, and I forgot all about it. I had spotted a squirrel in a nearby palm tree, and he was much more interesting.

When we came home, mom took the ring from her pocket and washed it in the kitchen. Then she applied some white paste on it and cleaned some more. It became so shiny! I got an extra treat for finding it. Mom said it was valuable and old. She said it had an inscription inside, and it looked like a wedding ring.

Later in the afternoon she went to her computer and posted something on the web. She kept looking at the ring, and said she was hoping to find the owner.

Again, I forgot all about it, until a couple of days later when mom got a call on her cell phone. She got excited, and I overheard her telling someone about how I found the ring. She was saying, "yes, yes, the inscription reads exactly like that, Anna & Thomas 6/26/1948!" She talked to that person for a long while, and she was smiling when she finished the call. She told me and dad that she had located the owner of the ring! The call was from the daughter of a woman named Anna Smith, who had lost her wedding ring on a family picnic in the mid-1970s in that very park. She said it was amazing that the ring had been buried there for almost 40 years, and that I had dug it up! She told me that the woman was now 83 years old and had been living in an assisted living facility for the last two years after her husband Thomas died. Mom said the woman wanted to see me too. We would go to see her the next day.

In the morning the next day, mom brushed me thoroughly with the strawberry-scented dry shampoo, so my coat became all soft and fluffy. She cleaned my ears and brushed my teeth too. I was looking and smelling my best, very representable! Then we went to see the old woman.

After almost an hour's ride, we stopped in front of a white apartment building with a wooden carved sign that read "Evening Sun" on the gate. Mom carried me on her shoulder. We went into the reception and got directions to Anna's apartment. We took the elevator to the third floor and stopped in front of the door where it said "Apt 312 Smith." An old lady came to open the door. Her hair was completely white, and she walked a little bent using a walking stick to assist her. She smiled and she looked friendly. I sensed a lot of kindness emanating from her, and I liked her immediately.

Anna invited us into her cozy apartment. It had a small kitchenette that opened to a small living space where she had a sofa and two easy chairs around a table. The furniture was old but well kept. She also had a shelf with lots of framed pictures. Some of them were old with no color and some were newer. As soon as we sat down, mom took out a small box from her purse and gave it to Anna. Her hands were shaking a little when she opened it, and then tears started streaming down her wrinkled cheeks. She took the ring and put it on her finger. She cried and smiled at the same time. She looked at the ring and touched it many times. It was a little big for her now, she said she had lost some weight after her husband died.

Then she made coffee. She invited us to the balcony where she had a table and some chairs. She brought out cookies and coffee cups. She and mom enjoyed the coffee, and I enjoyed the cookies! They were so good. Then the old lady invited me to jump into her lap, and I did! She hugged me and kissed the top of my head. It was absolutely wonderful. I sensed so much love and gratitude! My little heart was as full of happiness as hers. She petted me and told mom that she and her husband Tom always had dogs when they still lived in their house. She said she was so delighted to see me. I had found her original wedding ring, and I was her hero.

Anna and mom talked for a long while. Anna told mom about her wedding in Philadelphia in 1948, just after her Tom returned from the war in Europe. She went on telling us about their children and how they used to vacation in Florida. Her life story was interesting. She had seen so much. I felt all warm and fuzzy being able to give her some comfort and happiness.

When we were about to leave, Anna asked mom if we could come visit her again. One of her daughters lived fairly close and came to see her once a week, but she was very busy, Anna said. The other daughter lived up north and came only a few times a year. Anna said she was happy to get visitors, including furry ones like me. Mom promised we'd come again next month.

Finding the treasure and visiting Anna turned out to be the beginning of what would become my calling in life. I didn't quite know it yet, but I had an inkling that these developments were significant in some way.

36 MOM TRAVELS TO AFRICA

Today is not a good Sunday. Mom is going on a work trip. How do I know for sure? Her purple suitcase is open on the guest room bed. That's a sure sign. She calls it her little carry-on, but to me it looks huge. I jumped on the bed and checked it out. It's still empty, but soon mom will be running back and forth between her closet and her office. It's confusing. I can't keep up with her. That's when I know *it* is happening. She'll be traveling again.

Today she also opened *that* drawer in her office. That's where her black flight folder is. She checked her passport! Soon she'll print her ticket. She's so predictable. It's gonna be a *long* trip. I know because I pay attention. She prints several pages and then cuts out the boarding passes. I can count to five, but there are more of them! Many plane changes, a long trip for sure.

I know everything in the house, most of the time in advance. I sense things. I don't like surprises, other than new treats or toys. I'm expecting those surprises, so when I get them it's more like a dream come true. But do know that I'm always genuinely grateful. Mom says my tail goes 50 miles an hour when I'm happy, but now I'm not. I think I'll put my tail between my legs shortly so mom will notice I don't like what I see.

I mentioned my dreams. Yes, I dream a lot. Mostly it feels good. Sometimes I sense my feet working the running motion on the bed, and sometimes I bark loud. I wonder if it sounds as loud to mom and dad as it sounds to me or if they hear it just like a little whimper. That would be embarrassing. I almost never bark otherwise. Only when someone knocks on the door, or when I sense a bad person. I have to protect the house. I get paid for that. You know, food, walks, rubs and treats on a regular basis. I also get lots of love, but I consider that more like a swap. Love for love. I think I'm giving more, but who counts. It feels good to have a positive balance on that.

Anyway, I wonder if there is anything I could do to get mom to stay at home. Maybe I should run to the deli and buy a lotto ticket? I've seen people buy them so I'm sure they win money. Why would they buy them otherwise? Then I could give bags of money to mom, and she wouldn't need to travel for work anymore. Or I could fake an illness, like collapsing on the floor and holding my breath, but that's not me. I could never do that. It's not honest. I'm an honest dog, and I'm trusted. No pretending here, you get what you see. And I'm mature, such pranks are not for someone almost ten years old.

Then mom takes me on her lap and starts explaining things. She knows that I'm no longer used to her weekly travels, so every time she plans to travel she explains things to me, like "mom needs to go to work again." That's funny since I see her working almost every day in her office. I sit right next to her or in her lap when she talks on the phone and types away on her laptop. So why does she say she needs to go to work? Why travel when she can work here at home, like any other day? She tells me she's going to travel to Africa for a week. She has clients there who want to see her. Now I'm thinking why not use Skype? These things are so difficult to understand. Mom says she'll be back after seven days and six nights. I can count to five, so it'll just be one more night, right?

Maybe I have to face it. Mom will be gone tomorrow, and I bet it'll be early. That means I'll need to cuddle with dad, but he's not mom. He gives me treats though and real man-sized portions of food. I have to watch my weight with him so mom doesn't think I'm fat when she comes home. I don't want to be put on a diet. *One bone a day keeps the doctor away* is not for me. I'm happy you didn't see me smile, since my two front *teeff* are missing.

I hope I can talk with mom on the phone. Dad hasn't allowed that since the time I stopped eating for two days after talking to mom, but that's long ago now. I was childish then, not *mature* like now. I hope he's forgotten that little incident. *Dad, I will not stop eating if you allow me to talk to mom, please!* Otherwise I'll have to ask for a doggy phone. I saw one online, but I'm usually not in to things that are unnecessary or just plain trendy.

I also hope mom doesn't take her laptop. I might be able to jump up on her office chair and do some interesting research while she's gone.

I would get used to these occasional trips to far locations. Mom said they are her window to the world, whatever that means. I'm content with the big windows we have at home. I can see the birds and the squirrels out there, in my world.

37 DOGGY FASHIONS

The days are long when mom is traveling. Dad's not much for going anywhere when he's alone with me. I've been trying to tell him that this is the time to go on an adventure, man to man, but he's not listening. He's glued to his TV and his computer most of the time, and the walks we take are shorter than with mom. It's been truly boring for the last few days. I've counted five and one more nights since mom left. I wish I could have gone to see my friend Anna at the Evening Sun.

Dad has been in mom's office and he left the door ajar. That's good! I'm jumping up into mom's office chair. I see mom took the small netbook with her so her laptop is right here for me to use! I'm thinking of getting my own blog. I already know I don't need to pay for it. It's all free. It would be a tightly focused, educative blog. I've already thought of a good domain name for it: "How to Train Your Humans." I admit it's a slightly sensitive topic, but I'm positive there would be a great interest for it among the dogs in the blogging world. I once talked to mom about it, but *noffing* has happened on that front. Maybe she didn't like the idea?

In any case, now she's away and dad really doesn't follow me everywhere, so I'm sitting in mom's office chair and flipping the pages on the internet. I'm looking at doggy fashions! Not that I'm into fashion, on the contrary. I passionately dislike all the funny costumes mom sometimes tries to put on me. I look so ridiculous! If I was to wear something, it would be real clothes, like people have. I see myself that way. But it's fun to see what's out there. You know, what other guys are wearing, particularly up north.

Oh, here is somebody similar to Tashi, the Tibetan terrier I told you about earlier. He's wearing a yellow raincoat with a hood and all. It covers his head, his whole back and part of his tummy too. The rain gear looks good, but must be uncomfortable. How do you lift your back leg when the stiff, heavy material hangs right there? It's likely to be a bit messy.

My cousin Pebbe also has a raincoat. I've seen a picture of him walking in that creation! It was a full body coverall of silver-colored, thin material with dark blue socks reaching down to his paws. Oh my, I could never wear anything like that. It looked good on him though. He's a handsome larger poodle, and he's into modeling! You better believe me. You know, when the fall fashions for doggies come out in September, he's always showing the new gear in magazines and stuff. That's right, he's a dog on the cat walk!

I see Smart Pet is already advertising for Halloween costumes, and it's not even September! They seem to start earlier and earlier every year. I see the Spiderman dog, the funny-bunny dog and the pumpkin dog! I've never seen anything more ridiculous. Why would any dog voluntarily put on these things? I don't get it. Like when Amelia was clad as a tiny mouse one Halloween. A mouse! She must have gotten loads of treats for doing that, but that's not for me. No way. I could imagine being a scary, huge rat or something else equally frightening. Maybe.

Oh, I almost forgot. Mom will be coming home tonight. I can't wait! I always take her out for a refreshing walk, no matter how late she comes home. She needs the exercise after sitting in the plane for hours and then driving home from the airport. I think I'll just sit at the door from now on and wait.

I have to smile at myself. The future would show that I had to learn to be more flexible and not always stick to my quickly formed opinions to the letter.

38 GOING BOATING

One other thing that I love about living in Florida is access to the ocean. Don't get me wrong, I'm not a big swimmer in general, but I like to go boating. And when we do, we all swim, including me.

We have a small boat. Dad says it's too small to go far away from the shore, or to be out in stormy weather, but I think it's just right for us! I don't like deep sea fishing anyway, and going out there when the waves are topping three feet is not pleasant. I could easily get seasick. My tummy could turn upside down, and that would not be pleasant for anybody onboard.

I love the little trips we do. I get to wear my blue life vest and my ears flap in the wind. The faster we go the better! Once I wanted to go tubing. You know, when a mattress is pulled after the boat. Mom said she couldn't tie me onto the mattress tight enough for me to stay on it when the boat speeds. I was a bit disappointed, but then I saw a young guy do it. I think mom was right. The mattress hit hard on the waves, bounced up and down, flew sideways and there were a ton of bubbles! It was fun to watch, but maybe I was better off sitting on the boat.

I love to go to this one particular island. It's uninhabited and few people ever go there. It has shallow white beaches, and the sand is soft. My family likes the crystal clear water, and we spend hours snorkeling. This is where I also go into the water to swim and snorkel. It's such a wonderful beach. We always find large white sand dollars and other treasures from the bottom of the sea. I haven't found out whether or not these dollars can buy doggy toys in Smart Pet yet, but I know they're valuable.

Last time we were there we got a surprising visitor, completely unannounced. We were all swimming and suddenly mom was screaming. I thought she'd been bitten by a big fish, like a shark or something. I was ready to swim to her rescue! Then I looked more carefully and saw a large dolphin. They are nice, intelligent animals and not fish. Mom had told me that earlier when we saw two of them swimming ahead of our boat. This one was swimming around mom, who was now standing waist deep in the water. She had been a bit scared when the dolphin first came to nudge her, but now she was delighted. The dolphin stayed with us for a while and then swam out to the ocean. The whole experience was very special.

Another thing that I love about these small outings is that we usually go out in the morning and return just before sundown. That means lunch on the beach somewhere, and I mean an excellent lunch on the beach. Mom never brings my bowl or my food, so I get what they get. Usually chargrilled chicken breasts or yummy sausages! I love the lunch time on these trips. I get pieces from everyone, and no one keeps a count. That's what I call a picnic! I'm suggesting we make a small boating trip a regular feature in the weekend calendar, every week. No one would ever be bored.

I still think these trips are wonderful. Unfortunately we don't go out as often as I would like simply because mom and dad have so many other things to do.

39 LABOR DAY LABOR

Today is Labor Day. Mom told me, and she knows almost everything. I'm wondering what this holiday is all about. First I thought this was a day when people volunteered to do labor, you know, like helping others. After our visit to that old lady, Anna, I'm thinking of doing exactly that, volunteering. But many people seem to be off from work today, not doing any labor. That is if we don't count laying in the sun on the beach as labor. But maybe it is?

It's hot today. It must be laborious to get up from those little beach chairs. They seem to sink into the sand pretty fast. Then the people have to walk to the ocean to cool off. Swimming is hard work, not easy to stay afloat unless you move all your paws vigorously. I've been there, done that. Then they have to fetch drinks. I see them digging into those big boxes with wheels. Some people seem to do that often, and all of them are balancing big plastic mugs. When they get up, some of them are so exhausted they can't walk straight. It must be hard work.

There is so much drama going on. I've heard the sirens of emergency vehicles far too many times this weekend. You should've seen last night. Just when mom and I were quietly strolling along the sidewalk, I got the scare of my life! I heard brakes squeal and then a real loud bang-bang, right next to us! *So scary.* Of course I had to go and inspect what happened.

Three cars had tried to go on top of each other, I think. Anyway, that's how it looked from my viewing angle, and that's not good. Luckily there were no dogs in any of the cars, and the people came out by themselves in one piece. Afterwards you should have seen the activity. So many red and blue lights. My poor eyes were hurting so we turned and came back home, but I wonder why those things happen on a straight street where cars can't even go fast. At least mom says so when I ask her to speed up so my ears would flap harder. Maybe these people just didn't pay attention or had been working too hard while on the beach?

Now I have to google. Mom says that she googles everything she doesn't know, which must not be a lot, but I wish she would google "the best dog massages." To tell you the truth, she's skilled in giving me massages, but sometimes she forgets my ears. I love ear massage. Oh, I almost forgot. I need to google "Labor Day."

Mom was right again, Google knows everything! Here we go: "Labor Day, the first Monday in September, is a creation of the labor movement and is dedicated to the social and economic achievements of American workers. It constitutes a yearly national tribute to the contributions workers have made to the strength, prosperity, and well-being of our country."

There it is. I hope everyone reads it, but I'm a little disappointed. That language is not easy to understand. I know what well-being means. It's when you have a bowl full of soft chicken stew, filtered water in the other bowl, you have an obedient companion for regular exercise, a warm lap to snuggle in and a soft bed for a good night's sleep. Oh, I should say a large bed, more like half of a king. So I can sleep in any direction. Straight, across and sideways.

I also know what dedicated means. Mom says she dedicates so much time to me. Why not all the time? The woman in my first house didn't want to dedicate any time to me; she left me in the shelter on that Christmas Eve. I was a young boy then, but one doesn't forget those things. Forgive yes, forget no. Now don't you forget what Labor Day is all about. I hope people do the right thing and celebrate responsibly.

Now I need to take mom for her midday walk, but we're not going to the sidewalk. We're going to watch squirrels, and I'm going to talk to her. She needs to know that I want to start working. I don't mean like earning money. Money is not important, happiness is, and I want to start giving happiness to older people who don't have many visitors, like Anna. I got that thought when we visited her last summer, and now is a good time to talk to mom about it. She needs to help me to make it happen. That will be my labor of love, and it's good to get going at it on Labor Day.

It's good to pause once in a while and just ponder about things. Those Labor Day musings proved to be an important starting point for my future endeavors.

40 I'M A VOLUNTEER!

When mom wants to make something happen, she usually gets it done. She liked my idea of visiting lonely, mature adults to give them some joy and encouragement. She liked it to the point that she called the old lady, Anna, to discuss whether or not she thought it was a good idea. To mom's surprise Anna had already thought about the same thing!

You see, after we returned her wedding ring, Anna had told several of her friends at the Evening Sun about our visit. All of them told her that they missed the company of the dogs they used to have as well, and they asked Anna if they could meet me when we visited again. It was perfect! I felt that I had found my calling, a small way to pay back a little of the good fortune bestowed on me, the rescue dog. I felt so excited!

A few days later mom told me we would be going to Anna's building to see her and a few of her friends. I felt a little bit nervous because I didn't quite know what was expected of me, but then I told myself to calm down. I would just be myself, nothing more or nothing less. That would do.

So finally yesterday afternoon, a day after my grooming appointment with Harold, we drove to visit Anna again. She was delighted to see me, and it was mutual! I felt like jumping up and down and walking on my two feet when I saw her old, loving face again. She was truly happy to see me, and I jumped right into her lap. She gave me a kiss on my fluffy head and said she had missed me. She also said she had felt rejuvenated after our last visit. She had started to take walks again in the afternoons and joined a bridge group in her building. It was wonderful to hear.

After a while two of her friends came in. Anna had invited them for coffee and cookies, and to meet me. Both ladies were sweet, and they told me they used to have dogs. One of them last had a poodle and the other had a Rottweiler. They are big dogs! I can't play with a Rottweiler even if I try to, the pounds will just not add up. I greeted both ladies and then ended up in their laps, both in turn. I got ear massages and long belly rubs, and I really felt the good vibes in the room. It was a warm and enjoyable atmosphere. All three old ladies were wonderful. We chatted for a long while, and I'm sure mom had three cups of coffee. I only had a few cookies. I hope no one counted.

After a couple of hours Anna asked us whether we would like to visit her friend who lived on the second floor. She told us his name was Rainier, and he was almost bed ridden at the moment after his hip replacement surgery. He could only get out of the bed when the physiotherapist came around. I told mom I was okay with a little visit.

Anna came with us to Rainier's apartment. It was similar to Anna's and homey. Rainier spoke with a slight French accent. He was charming, although he must have been in pain. He tapped his hand on his bed, like inviting me to jump up, and so I did. I curled up against his side, and he was petting me. He said he was so happy to see me. He used to have a Dalmatian named Charlie, and he missed Charlie a lot. So there I was, feeling all warm and fuzzy. I saw a little tear trickle down Rainier's cheek. He said it was from happiness and not because he was sad. When we left, I made *Monsieur* Rainier promise me that he would be up on his feet the next time we visited. He laughed and said he certainly would.

Mom and I spent the whole afternoon in that building. It was one of the best days of my life. I wanted it to become my other work, in addition to protecting my home. Volunteering to cheer up others was awesome! Mom agreed to help me with making that happen. Now I had become Bumble the volunteer!

And so indeed it happened. I have visited the assisted living facility about once a month from that day on. Some of my friends there have moved on to become angels in heaven over the past few years, and new friends have arrived. Anna is still there, going strong at 87! That is so lovely, and the work itself is rewarding. I feel younger every time I come home from there. My work has since expanded to other areas, as you'll learn later. It's a blessing!

41 HALLOWEEN

In my first house, I was never allowed to participate in Halloween festivities. I was always locked into the basement so that I would not disturb the trick 'r treating activities. That house was in an older neighborhood, and lots of kids came to our door. Elisa and the woman used to wear costumes, different ones for every year, but I hated this holiday, simply because I was always excluded.

But things are different in my real home. Mom's son is big now and lives in his own home, but mom always buys treats for the neighborhood kids who come and knock on the door. Last year she got an idea. Have I told you that mom always has new ideas? I don't know where they all come from, but I have to say that some are good, like letting me sleep on the king bed on my red blanket, but others are not so good. As seen from my vantage point, of course.

So this idea was to get me a costume for Halloween. It was a little cape with skulls on it and a weird witch hat. The cape was okay because it left my feet free to move under it, but the hat was a real nuisance. It tipped over my eyes all the time. Since my eyesight is not so good to start with, I need to have an unrestricted view at the minimum. That hat didn't stay on for too long.

Then mom put me to be the first one at the door when she opened it. She stayed behind the door so it appeared as if I had opened the door by myself. She had made a small "purse" to hang from around my neck. I stood up on my two feet and kids helped themselves to the treats, mostly individually wrapped mini chocolates.

Anyway, you already know that I don't like to wear clothes. But actually last Halloween it was different. The trick 'r treating kids were amused to see the "devil dog." They laughed and petted me. They told their friends, and more kids came to our door. More back scratching and petting my head. "He's *soooo* sweet" was the comment I heard almost every time someone was treated. So I thought that this costume was different, it was more tolerable. I could actually wear it for a few hours, and I was wondering if mom would ask me to use the same costume this year or if we would go out to buy a new one.

I didn't need to wait for the answer for too long. This morning mom came to me with a face that could only mean one thing: here is something for you to try on! She had a small bag, and she let me peek into it. The small garment looked like pajamas, with four legs and a hood of some kind! Mom took it out and spread it on the sofa in her office. It was a lambkin costume with a cute head, a body and four legs. It even had a little pocket for my tail and a zipper up on my back. OMG! I could not become a little lamb...that was out of the question. This costume was even worse than Amelia's little mouse costume!

I told mom so, and I asked her why on earth she would buy a new costume without consulting me. She just smiled and said I would be the cutest little lambkin opening the door this year. Yeah right! If any of the neighborhood dogs were on their evening walk when I stood there in the lit doorway as a lamb, the whole neighborhood would know. I would never be able to go near the dog park again.

Mom looked a little dejected, and I felt bad. In my heart I didn't want to disappoint her. So I decided to do something that I do well. I would negotiate. I would put on that costume tonight provided that (1) mom took me on a long ride in the car tomorrow for the same amount of time as my lamb duty lasted tonight; (2) mom would check that absolutely no dogs were on the street when she opened the door; (3) that next year she would take me to Smart Pet and we would select the costume together; and (4) I would get a thorough massage tonight after putting on this show.

To my amazement mom agreed. I realized that I could have asked for more, but I'm not like that. I have a good character. I tried on the costume, and it fit perfectly. I looked at myself in the hall mirror, and I have to admit I looked like a lambkin. Very cute. Did you hear the irony in my voice?

So now the little lamb is waiting for the first kids to arrive. Let's get this Halloween party going so we can enjoy the comprehensive massage afterwards.

It went well! No neighborhood dogs saw me, I got my massage and the car ride that mom promised. She keeps her promises, and so do I. It's a trademark of a good dog.

42 BOXING DAY

It's Christmas evening, the second in my new home, and I am now almost 11 years old, I mean young! I hope it's not too late to say Merry Christmas? It's all continuing tomorrow, on Boxing Day, right?

Anyway, I'm just sending friends belated Season's Greetings, taking advantage of the fact that mom and dad have gone to bed early tonight. It's different from yesterday, let me tell you! Food, presents, hugs, friends, food, Swedish glögg, Christmas songs by Elvis and Louis Armstrong. Then more food. It was lively, and it was late! In mom and dad's European tradition, Christmas Eve is the day for a big Christmas dinner, presents and fun, then Christmas Day is more for quiet contemplation in joy and gratitude. After moving here to America they are trying to adapt their traditions a little bit. Like putting up and taking down the Christmas tree much earlier, and also having some presents on Christmas morning. It's a little bit confusing, I know, but that's how it is.

I sat in the easy chair in the living room the whole evening. Better to be out of the way. I mean, whenever I wasn't getting belly rubs or helping out in the kitchen. You know, carving the ham and the turkey, or helping with the desserts.

Nowadays I love Christmas. Particularly the food part and the gifts. This year I got a new leash, one that blinks in the dark so the drivers can see us whenever I need to take mom across the street on her evening walk. I also got a bag of yummy bacon-wrapped biscuits and a new toy fox. It doesn't look new anymore, of course. It was a long night.

This morning everybody went to church for Christmas Mass. As you may know, they don't allow dogs in the church, so I had some quiet time for myself. I used it to contemplate and to be grateful for everything I have. I've learned that good thoughts, like being thankful, will bring along good things, so I try to do my part. I must confess that while they were gone I also took a much needed short nap.

Every Christmas mom makes me put on a Santa costume. After putting up with these pageants for a few years, I finally had a heart-to-heart with her about it last year. I thought she got it, but I was wrong. Earlier this month, when she took the decorations up from the storage room, I saw the red Santa costume reappear. She hadn't gotten rid of it. So yesterday, on Christmas Eve, when she came to me with the costume in her hand, I gave her the *look*. You know, the one for *didn't we discuss this already?* But she just smiled innocently and offered to help me put it on. I didn't have the heart to disappoint her and the little Princess.

Now the costume is on the blue sofa again. I may need to plan a play session with my fox so that we just happen to step on it a few times. Repeatedly. If that doesn't do the trick, I may need to put on more weight during the year so that I can't fit into it next year. That shouldn't be too hard, provided that mom cooperates. You know, provides me with enough to eat. None of us wants to see that ridiculous costume next year. I hope I'm right.

But you know, all in all, it's been a wonderful holiday season so far, and tomorrow is only the 26th, Boxing Day. The feast continues at least until after the New Year, right?

That reminds me that we will go to see our friends at Evening Sun again before the New Year. I really look forward to those trips. I hope mom has made some presents for all my many friends there, like framed pictures of me in their lap. That would be nice.

Yes, that was indeed a wonderful Christmas! We went to visit our friends right on Boxing Day and the Christmas spirit continued for many days.

43 I'M A HAPPY BLOGGER!

Mom is reading blogs again. She is an avid blogger and has quite a following. I think it means people subscribe to what she writes, but she says she doesn't get any money out of it, so her writings cannot be that good.

Oh, now mom went to the kitchen. It's lunch time and she'll be busy for a while. The laptop is all mine, and the WordPress page is open. I can't believe my luck! It's now or never. First I have to log mom out. Done. Now I'll go ahead and register my new blog. I have reconsidered the domain name. To talk about training humans might get me into hot water and colleagues may not dare to subscribe. Some of their humans are strict and might think my blog will put wrong ideas in the heads of their dogs. I'd better come up with something more neutral, quickly. Hmm, how about "Wise Advice from Bumble-boy?" I think that's clever. With a nice picture of me, the blog could attract both males and females, I think.

Where's the camera? I'll need to snap a quick picture for my *Gravataff*. Oh, there we go. Click. My nose looks huge in the picture. I guess it was closest to the camera eye. This picture is definitely not perfect. Mom always says that perfect is the enemy of good, and I'm a good boy, so it'll have to do.

My readers will need to like and follow me for the quality of my writing, not because I look handsome or cute.

I could give advice on a wide variety of topics, such as delicious diets, the best toys, how to exercise your humans, and why not a few words on how to train them as well? Once in a while I could even touch upon more serious matters, such as finding your true calling or the importance of maintaining a positive attitude. I could even give advice on matters of love. That would make it even more exciting.

Oh, here we go. Now I have a domain name. I'll just start typing away while mom is still busy. I'll begin with a welcome post. I've seen many bloggers use quotes at the beginning of their posts. Sometimes the quote is the only thing in the post, maybe with a picture. Go on. Read my welcome post and say what you think. You're free to comment, I won't edit anyone's comments, I promise. Unless they are negative. We don't like to dwell on negativity on this blog. We want to inspire.

Welcome!

"In order to really enjoy a dog, one doesn't merely try to train him to be semihuman. The point of it is to open oneself to the possibility of becoming partly a dog." - Edward Hoagland

I love that quote! It expresses so perfectly what this blog is all about. This blog will give life insights and useful advice to both dogs and their humans. We need to understand each other and learn from each other in order to optimally benefit from our close relationship.

You can read all about me on the "About" page, but to make a long story short, I can tell you that I am Bumble, a toy poodle, and I am a rescue dog. I have seen so much of life, good and bad, that I feel it's time to share my experiences and the wisdom I have accumulated in my first eleven years. You will learn to know me better as our journey together advances. I am planning to post something at least once a week, or whenever I get uninhibited access to mom's laptop.

I hope you will follow me and get all new posts directly into your own inbox. That inbox will become like a food bowl for you. You go there regularly to get food for thought, and I hope you will comment on my

posts. That's how we can build an interesting and interactive community of happy dogs. Comments from humans are welcome as well. We want to benefit from diverse views. They enrich the discussion.
Have a great day and I'll see you shortly.
Oh, and now I'm pressing the "publish" button. It's a bit scary to have my voice out there for everyone to read. What do you think? Oh, I got my first star right away! It means that someone already liked my post. I'll need to come back later to see how it's going. Now I'll log out so mom doesn't see my blog. I'll show it to her later when I get a few postings done, so that she can see I'm not dreaming. Now I finally have my own blog!

Looking back on that day, I must say that starting my own blog was a huge step for me. It has helped me to learn to write, including finally daring to embark on writing this book!

44 MY PHOTO ALBUM

Today I became a bit nostalgic. I was looking through my photo collection. As you may guess, I have no photos from my first four years, the time I spent in my first house. It's really sad, but I accept it for what it is. Nobody can change the past. Now I consider the first pictures taken after I met mom and dad as pictures from my youth. I was almost four when I came to my real home from the shelter. My life after that has been great, and I have lots of photos to remind me! You know, me as a youngster, me in the bath, me playing hide and seek with squirrels, me driving mom's car, me and the little Princess, me and mom. There's also pictures of all my friends: Amelia, Tashi, Pebbe, and my Canadian friend Sam.

As you already know, Amelia is a beautiful white Chihuahua girl, who now lives in north Florida. We get along well, at least when she isn't trying to prevent me from eating my food, licking *my dad* behind his ear or diving into *my mom's* bed under the covers. Yes, she is wonderful, most of the time, and I miss her. I hope she'll visit soon again, or we get to drive to see her and the little Princess.

Tashi is also a good friend of mine, although he still lives up north in Maryland. He's handsome and everybody calls him King Tashi! He *loves* winter and snow. His breed comes from Tibet and I guess he's lucky because they seem to have so many blizzards up in Maryland nowadays. A foot of snow in half a day is a Tashi kind of winter! He runs in the snow, digs in the snow, and he likes his sturdy winter clothes. When I lived up there I hated the snow. I couldn't find any grass to pee on, and the cold would bite me even under my curly coat.

Tashi told me that it's too hot for him in the summertime, like a sauna. He always hopes the fall will come soon since he loves to jump around in the huge piles of leaves his mom rakes up. He loves the rain too! He has so many different types of clothes for all types of weather. I told him that here in Florida we all go naked all the time! He was horrified, and I got myself a good laugh. He is so proper. We're different, but we have so much to learn from each other.

My cousin Pebbe who lives much further up north is more similar to me, just bigger. He's a miniature poodle. Miniature! He is huge compared to me, and a youngster. He's about five, I think, hardly out of his diapers. He loves to travel! He just came back from a cruise with his parents. He told me that he loved the cruise ship. Unlike many such ships lately, they had no problems with power. He could watch TV and his toilet worked all the time! Pebbe told me he was carefully monitoring the journey from his state-room window. I've only met him on Skype, and we're Facebook buddies, but we like each other and chat a lot. I hope he comes to visit us sometime soon. I can't wait until he shows the fall fashions for poodles again!

Then I found a lot more pictures of myself as a young man, four and five or so. It's a pity that dieting is so hard nowadays! I don't have much hope of getting back to the feather-weight series. Well, one has to enjoy what the good life has to offer. Especially the treats, but I have to confess that I get sentimental every time I sit and look at the pictures in my album.

This album is still one of my best treasures. I sit and look at the photos every time I miss someone.

45 GRANNIES AND KIDS

I have to give you an update on how my volunteering is going. Actually, it's not only going well, but it has expanded and become more formalized! It's true. In addition to my friends at the Evening Sun, I am now also visiting the Children's Hospital once a month, and they call me Therapy Dog! It's a nice title that I didn't earn in medical school but in the hard school of life. I've learned to stay calm and positive despite the obstacles that life has thrown at me.

You know, last month when I visited my oldest friend Anna, she asked me if I liked children. I told her I do! Mom told her about the incredible bond that has developed between me and our little Princess. She smiled and told me that her great grandson was in the Children's Hospital after he had a bad accident when riding his bike. His leg was badly broken and had needed surgery. Now he had to stay in the hospital for a while, and he might need more surgery as well. Anna asked me if I'd care to visit him. I looked at mom, and she nodded. She said we would go there as soon as we would get permission from the hospital.

So the next day mom contacted the hospital and did lots of research on how I could become certified as a therapy dog. Going to see Anna and her friends was a good start, but it was all informal. Going to see sick kids in a hospital was a different matter. Anyway, to make a long story short: I passed the test and the observed field visits went really well. In just two weeks I got registered as a therapy dog! I didn't quite know what that meant, but mom explained that a therapy dog was a well behaved, obedient and patient dog, who helped people to feel happier so they would also feel better soon. Good enough for me. That's exactly what I have been trying to do for a long time.

After breakfast this past Monday, we jumped into mom's car and drove into the city. Once there we went into a huge building. It had too many stories for me to count them. In the reception we had to show our credentials. I got an additional small tag on my harness. It said, "Therapy Dog, Children's Hospital."

We rode several different elevators and walked many corridors. Finally we came to an area where some children were playing. They saw me, and all of them asked mom if they could pet me. Of course! That's why I was there. Little arms hugged me from all sides, someone scratched my ears, and all of them snuggled close by. My tail went 50 miles an hour! I was happy to make them forget their illness for a little while.

From the playroom we continued to the room of the little boy we were supposed to visit. The little boy's name was Jackson and he was about five years old I would guess. He was in his hospital bed with one of his legs in a cast and tilted upward. He could sit up, but he couldn't walk or run.

I jumped on his bed and sat close so he could pet me. He was so happy I saw a tear roll down his cheek. I snuggled close to him, and he petted me softly on my head with his little hands. He wanted to give me one of his chocolates, but mom told him I could not eat chocolates, I would get sick if I did. He understood.

Jackson showed me the toys he had in his room: a little car, some game gear, a little miniature tractor, a teddy bear and a few books. We started reading them together. I stayed until the boy fell asleep.

When mom and I left his room, we stopped by the playroom again. There were more kids than I could count, and they all came to pet me. Then a nice lady came in and she talked to mom. I heard her asking if we could visit these kids again. Yes, mom, let's come back even after Jackson has gone home, I tried to say, and mom seemed to agree. She promised to call in a couple of weeks to ask when it would be a good time to come back.

So that's how my volunteer work has expanded. I now have two places to visit, and I get paid richly. Or should I say my reward is priceless? All the little happy faces and all the old happy faces with sparkling eyes!

This was the beginning of my official work as a therapy dog. Better late than never, right?

46 TAKING CARE OF FITNESS

I have to confess that I didn't take enough care of my health when I was younger. In my first house, they didn't care about me too much, and I was too young to know better. My diet was horrible, and I didn't get much exercise. I got kibbles in my bowl every morning, but then I also got loads of sweets and candy every day. When you're young and foolish, you think candy is good for you. As a result of not taking care of my fitness, I became a couch potato, had little energy, weak muscles and my teeth got bad.

Luckily, that's history. Now I eat much better, and I exercise regularly. Of course, I still like my snacks and treats, but they are much healthier now. You see, a few weeks ago I changed my diet after my nice doctor recommended it to mom. I heard her say, "This little guy is gaining weight. He might be getting too many treats, and they have so many calories. Why don't you try to feed him carrots as snacks?" I pretended not to have heard anything. I loved my snacks and treats: the little milk bones with chicken, the tiny sausage rolls and the small picnic sandwiches. Every day I looked forward to snack time and wanted treats after our walks. I didn't really want to change anything. Everything was as it was supposed to be. A little "fast food" couldn't hurt anyone, right?

After coming home from the doctor's office we did our usual afternoon walk. It was a fairly short one because mom was in the middle of something work related. When we came back into the kitchen, I looked at mom as in *where's my Milkbone*, but she didn't open the pantry where my treats are. Instead, she went into the fridge and took out a small bag of tiny orange-colored sticks. She said they were baby carrots, and I would now have them as snacks and at treat time. *Don't be so sure.* I was suspicious. I didn't want to taste them, but mom didn't budge. She took a knife and cut the little round sticks into small round slices and put them into my food bowl.

The color looked good, almost like Halloween candy, but I knew that after all the problems with my teeth, mom would never give me candy. If that was all I would get, maybe I should taste. Carefully, just one little round slice. *Crunch, crunch.* I had to bite it, I couldn't just swallow! That was different. I tasted fruit sugar. *Hmm.* Had to crunch another one. Not too bad. Had to taste one more, and another after that. Oh, I had eaten all of them! I guess they were ok after all.

So that's how easily I embarked on a healthier diet. I checked the pantry and my usual treats are no longer there. I feel my weight has already dropped a little bit. It's easier to run, my step is lighter somehow. It's easy to change gears from walking to running, and it feels good!

I have to tell you that my exercise routine is much more multifaceted than just walking mom four times a day. First of all, I play a lot. After every meal I chase my rabbit, my fox and my squirrel. I push them ahead of me pretending they are running away, and then I catch them and play with them.

I've invented a new exercise that I have to tell you about. I take the fox in my mouth and jump up on mom and dad's bed. Then I lay down close to the end of the bed to play. I push the fox little by little closer to the end of the bed, and then onto the footboard itself. From there it always jumps down on the floor! It has nowhere else to run. Then I also jump down and chase it, and then we jump up together again! Repeat at least two sets of ten jumps. I call that an excellent workout. Jumping more than one's height certainly burns calories! I wish mom would buy me one of those little calorie counters so that I would know when to stop. Without that helpful device I may accidentally burn too many calories, and then I'll have to eat something again.

And of course I run a lot. First, I run as fast as mom can walk. Then I run alone too. I'm supposed to stay in the yard, but sometimes when mom takes a power nap in the lounge chair, I run out and take a power trip to the shopping center and back along the sidewalk. I always check if Carmen is working in the little deli. She's my friend, and I always get a nice belly rub from her! People here all know me, you see. No one is surprised to see me run in my full gear. They know I'm into sports, and that I would never run away from home.

The only thing I don't like about fitness is the fitness center itself in our big building. They have still not agreed to allow me there, even in mom's company. I've been in there briefly, and I saw so many interesting things, but there is one thing I don't get. Why do people run on the treadmill? They run and run but they don't get anywhere. If they want to watch the little TV, they could just stand there and watch. So things being as they are, it's in my interest that mom exercises at home as much as possible.

I may have already mentioned Pilates? That's my favorite. It's easy to do at home. Mom and I stretch and *streeeetch*. Front legs first and then the back legs, neck and the head too. We stretch the whole body. Once I have done my exercises for the day it's nice to just sit on the sofa, watch TV and wait for my dinner. With a good conscience.

Now that I'm getting a bit up in years, I appreciate the importance of taking care of fitness even more. I can still run and move much better than many friends of my age and I know it is because my body is used to being in motion.

47 JUST A LITTLE MISCHIEF

Don't you start to think that my life became boring or anything like that after I started my serious career as a therapy dog. On the contrary. I appreciate life even more now, and I am having lots of fun! Just to give you one example of living life to the fullest, I have to tell you about my cousin Pebbe's visit last week.

As I told you earlier, Pebbe and I had not met, other than via Skype, because he lives so far up north, but last week he finally came to visit me with his parents. *Wouff!* It was so much fun! We ran together in our garden chasing and watching squirrels. We didn't catch any, of course. That's not why we do it. It's all for fun, for both us and the squirrels.

One day we went to the nearby dog park together. I've only been there a couple of times previously because mom likes to walk close to the marsh where the birds live, and to tell you the truth, I haven't been too eager to go there either. I'm not too fond of being alone among the big dogs. You see, the park is divided into two parts; one is for the big dogs and the other for the small ones like me, but so many people can't read! They bring German shepherds and Rottweilers into the small dog park. They don't look small to me, but since Pebbe is a miniature poodle, although he is big compared to me, he could come to the small dog park with me. It was great.

We had become so close so quickly that we played some pranks on the other dogs. For example, we would suddenly run together like show dogs do, side by side, our heads high up and our fluffy, long ears flapping in the air. You should have seen the stare of the other dogs and their humans! Then we played cat walk. You will remember that Pebbe is a model, and he had taught me the type of walk they do when they present new doggy fashions. We made a little bit of a show out of it. We ran like models do, our paws in one straight line, stopped, then turned and ran back the same way. Mom and her sister applauded, and soon all humans were applauding to our fashion show without the fashions.

After all this showmanship, even the biggest dogs there seemed to like us, or they may have thought their humans liked us, so they had to behave. Whatever. The main thing was that no one tried to dominate us to boost their egos. That visit was so much fun!

Anyway, one day our moms and dads told us they would be going out for a long time. They were going to visit an art museum and other places, then they'd go out for a late lunch. They gave us a huge breakfast, and we took a long walk before they left.

I was actually looking forward to some nice time for just the two of us. You know, without constant supervision. Mom had left the TV on for us, so Pebbe took the seat in mom's tub chair, and I sat on the leather sofa. I demonstrated some serious channel surfing to my friend. There was no mistake: I was the master of the remote control! Finally we decided to watch the Disney channel. They had a marathon on Road Runner, you know the bird that always gets into trouble. He runs fast and unexpected things happen to him. We were laughing hard and holding our tummies!

But you can only watch cartoons so long. We got a little bored around lunch time and decided it was time to see what goodies mom had hidden in the kitchen pantry. I knew, of course, where the stash of my treats used to be, but I had not seen them there after I started my carrot diet. We opened the pantry door together. I can also do it alone, but it was much easier for two equally clever dogs to open it fast. Nice surprise! There was a little jar with Milkbones made of real chicken! I think mom had bought it just for Pebbe's visit. What a nice party we had!

Then we got thirsty. We had water of course, but who drinks plain water at a party? We opened the fridge. There was a milk carton in the door on the lowest shelf so we took it out. Pebbe told me that occasionally he would get to taste a milkshake when his mom made it for dessert. He knew it was a mix of milk and ice cream. I love ice cream, but nowadays we usually don't have ice cream at home because of my new diet, and because mom says she'll get fat if she eats it. I told Pebbe that we probably didn't have any ice cream, but we could check in the freezer.

After a few attempts we got the freezer door open! I could only see the two lowest shelves, and Pebbe could see three. No ice cream, but there were three more shelves that we couldn't reach. My little brain was working in high gear - and I had it! We should try to reach the upper shelves together, demonstrating real team work! So I asked Pebbe to lift me on his back, high up near his neck. After falling down a couple of times, I got the hang of it. He got up, standing on his back legs, and I stretched as high as I could! There it was! A huge container half full of vanilla ice cream. I stretched my paws and finally reached it. It tumbled right down on the kitchen floor. Victory! Team work was power!

So now we had both milk and ice cream. We had to act fast before the ice cream melted. I realized I should have planned this better and not been so spontaneous, acting before thinking, but it was too late to plan now. We just needed to act. From hanging so often on mom's shoulder, I knew that the blender was on the kitchen counter, at the very back wall. There was no way we could reach it there even if we were world champions of team work! Then I remembered I'd seen mom whisking eggs using a neat little handheld stick whisk. She kept it on the lowest shelf in the cupboard. I found it easily.

But the milkshake was not ours to taste if we couldn't find an electric outlet we could actually reach. The outlets were all up on the back wall, neatly planted into the new backsplash! We couldn't reach them, but then I remembered that I've seen mom sometimes charge her phone on the living room side of the breakfast bar! She always left the phone on a bar stool just because the outlet was placed so low. I quickly ran to check it out. Yes! The outlet was only a foot from the floor. Now we're talking!

We quickly hauled the whisk, the milk and the ice cream carton into the living room, next to the bar counter, and got into action. Pebbe poured some milk into the ice cream carton, and I plugged in the whisk. We both held the shaft, and I pressed the button. It worked! The whisk started turning in the ice cream and milk, faster and faster! *Shrrrrr. Splashhhh. Shrrrrr.* Some of the milk and the ice cream obviously wanted out of the carton. The sides weren't that deep after all, but we pressed on. One can't give up if one wants to get something good! Finally it all looked nice and smooth, I mean, what was remaining in the container. I pressed the button again and the whisk stopped. Now we had our milkshake!

Pebbe was right. It was good. We took turns drinking from the carton. Yummy! After all this enjoyment, we cleaned up the living room floor, and the side of the bar counter as well as we could. Some milk was dripping down from the bar stools, and we cleaned up that too. We hauled the milk back to the kitchen, next to the fridge door, and the whisk next to the dishwasher. Then we also cleaned the kitchen floor. One has to take care to be neat and clean up after a party. Mom had taught me that. Our party was a great success!

Then we both took a nap on the leather sofa until our parents came back home. I have to confess that there was a *smallish* aftermath to the party. Mom didn't look too happy when she came in, but then they all started laughing. She took her wet-jet and cleaned the floor again. I'm not sure why she had to do double duty, but I have to admit my paws felt kind of sticky when I walked on the tile floor. So maybe mom didn't like the sweet stickiness. She also wiped the bar stools and put everything away. She said we wouldn't get any treats because we had eaten almost all of them. We would return to my carrot diet immediately. My tummy was so full that I didn't want to get into a negotiation on such a small issue. Carrots would be good for me and for Pebbe too.

Now afterwards I realize how much I enjoyed Pebbe's visit. I hadn't had so much fun in a long time. It was a real mood booster!

48 MY SOLO VACATION

I've got something I'm itching to tell you. You know, last month there was a big festivity somewhere in Europe. I'm pretty sure Europe is far away because I've been everywhere that's close, and I've not been there. Mom said that although it wasn't work related, I couldn't go with her because dogs were not allowed to travel under the seat in the cabin on such long flights. I was disappointed, and honestly a little fearful. You wanna know why? Mom told me that because dad would also travel with her, I would have to go into a pet hotel and have my own vacation. I've never been in a pet hotel or boarding before if you don't count my stay at the shelter where mom and dad found me. So I didn't know what to expect.

I think mom was a bit nervous as well. Or was it guilt I smelled? She took me to visit several places where lots of dogs were staying in smaller or bigger "rooms." Everyone was trying to greet me. It quickly got lively and really loud! To tell you the truth, most places were not that homey and some were just big rooms full of crates. I think I was shivering a bit in mom's lap.

Finally we found a Pet Center that had a small house with only a few cozy "penthouse apartments" for small dogs. It was nice and quiet and more home-like. It was also next to an inviting exercise yard. The girls and guys who worked there were friendly. You know, I sensed they were real dog lovers. Right away they wanted to know my name, and petted me too. I gave mom a kiss. That was our secret sign that I had made my decision. This was a good place to stay.

A few days later, on a Saturday morning, mom packed my raised bowls, my red wool blanket, my black cat pillow, a few of my favorite toys, my food and my meds. I have to tell you that she was a little bit of a basket case, so I had to help her drive the car all the way to the Pet Center.

When we arrived there, I was greeted by a nice girl. Mom promised to come pick me up the following Friday. She said that more times than I could count. And as you know, I can count to five, plus one. Luckily those who worked there were trained in handling pet parents suffering from separation anxiety.

With all my stuff there, my little penthouse felt almost like home. It was warm and cozy, and I had nice neighbors. Like this one sweet Chihuahua girl. She was shy so she didn't talk a lot, but there was a rumor that she had won several beauty competitions when she was younger. No wonder with those gorgeous eyes of hers.

Soon I also got to go out to the little yard where I'd get my exercise. It was completely separate from the big dogs' yard, which was good. I have to say I came to enjoy my outings with the small ladies. They were all friendly, particularly this one Maltese girl. She was sweet and always happy. She made me smile and laugh to the point that I completely ignored my two missing front teeth! We played a lot in the grass, and I almost forgot I was supposed to miss mom! But don't tell her, *pleaff*.

I also loved that the girls and guys who worked there often let me hang around with them. One day I learned that some of the dogs were picked up every night and brought back again in the morning! I didn't see them over the weekend, so I think their parents might have been in adult daycare. One white-brownish Chihuahua girl caught my attention. She came in with her mom every morning sitting in a little red backpack. She reminded me so much of Amelia. You remember her, right?

Believe me when I say that life at the Pet Center was fun! There was so much happening every day. I never got bored and forgot all about my age! I felt rejuvenated.

I have to confess I never joined the swim club. I don't like to get wet, unless I can swim and snorkel in the ocean. My hair becomes such a curly mess. But many of my small neighbors loved splashing in the water several times a day. It was fun to observe. Good for them!

Time flew by fast. One morning I was taken to the building next to mine. It turned out to be the grooming salon. I guessed mom would come to get me soon. She always picks me up after a salon bath, and I was right! She came in as soon as I was dry and brushed. I felt a bit sad to leave all my new friends, but I was also excited and happy to go home. You know how it is when a vacation ends.

Okay, it's good to be home again. Now mom has to play with me, and believe me when I say I'm keeping her busy. But to tell you the truth, I wouldn't mind that much if there was another festivity in a faraway place at some point fairly soon. Now I know that a short vacation in a nice Pet Center can be totally cool!

Who would have known I'd have such great new experiences at my age!

49 INVENTIONS FOR DOGS

Have you ever thought about how many things have not yet been invented? I'm not sure about people things, but certainly there are many useful things that dogs would love to have if they had been invented. I wonder why that is. It might be because people put themselves first. They invent only stuff that is useful for them, such as the Dri Suit for their iPhones so that they can listen to music under water! Can you imagine? How is that more important than doggy dentures, for example? Or is it just that people don't think like dogs and simply haven't thought of the things we may need? I choose to think the latter. Most people would probably invent stuff for dogs if they could imagine what we might need.

So the other day I decided to do a simple poll on my blog. I described the items I had already thought of and asked my readers to vote on them. I also invited them to propose other things that I had not yet thought of. This is how I described the items I had already thought of:

Doggy dentures. Very much like dentures for humans but adapted to dogs with the right strength to bite through big bones and other hard stuff. Fastened by denture glue that tastes like chicken, preferably.

Doggy contact lenses. Useful to boost seeing for those of us whose eyesight, for whatever reason, was deteriorating. Eye glasses are not practical when we run after squirrels and play rough, but contacts that one can flip in with a swing of the paw would be great, and one should be able to nap and sleep with them too, like people do.

Bark Subwoofer. This would be especially useful for small dogs whose bark may not be powerful enough to scare away potential thieves and other shady characters. You would just bark into the subwoofer and it would sound like a Rottweiler or a Great Dane. You know, with really deep breast tones. You would also have an option to double the bark effect so that it sounds like two huge dogs are barking. An impressive and a cheap investment in home security.

Slip proof paw protectors. These would be like small pads in three sizes for big, medium and small dogs. One side would be adhesive, initially protected by a paper that you lick off, and the other side would be rough, a little bit like sandpaper. These protectors would be excellent on slippery wood or tile floors, and even on ice for our friends up north. In addition, they would also protect our paws from the heat on asphalted driveways in the summer here in the south.

Portable TV tablet for dogs. This would be a device that we could easily transport from room to room from a little handle bar, and it would use the Wi-Fi in the house. Such a device would allow us to watch TV through a dog friendly TV app on any couch or bed in the house. There could be a more expensive version with G4 doubling as a phone if we want to get in touch with our friends, or why not with mom when she's gone out to run errands? We may need to report on urgent security issues, for example.

Lazy Cat Teaser. This would be a handy toy for those of us who may have lazy cats in the household. You know, cats who just eat and sleep and don't take care of their chores. It would be a small tube holding a little toy mouse with an authentic look and smell. When you push a button, the mouse would "fly" in the air and land next to the cat. When the cat finally wakes up and realizes there is a mouse, you would push another button and the mouse would instantaneously retreat into the tube again. After seeing the mouse, the cat might be more willing to do his job, namely protecting the house from rats and mice. And maybe it would also want to play more, bonding a deeper friendship.

These were the items I had thought of already. My little poll got many responses and resulted in the Bark Subwoofer being a clear winner, followed by doggy contact lenses. All the other items shared third place. My readers came up with a few other inventions, but unfortunately the descriptions were not very specific. I have now written back to each of them asking for a synopsis of the look and functionality of their proposed devices, but I'll give you the rundown of their titles here: Doggy Back-Scratcher, Dri Suit for Dogs (I think that one was inspired by my writings), iBrushDog, an automatic tooth brush adapted for dogs, Thermo Bed with heated doggy mattress, Paw Operated Treat Feeder, Karaoke Machine for Dogs, and a Doggy Drum Set. I think the iBrushDog would be a great seller. You would just open your mouth and the teeth would brush themselves.

Anyway, I will submit a provisional patent application to protect my ideas. Then I will let the manufacturers compete for the license to actually make them. If this goes well, and I'm quite confident these items will sell like butter, the profits would go to my charities. The proceeds would pay for training and expenses for therapy dogs so that more kids and the elderly could enjoy their company on a regular basis. I would also help the shelters where homeless animals stay. I personally think this is a brilliant idea to secure more funding for such good purposes.

I still think these inventions are great. I am now in the process of preparing the specifications and writing my provisional patent applications. I'm hoping that by this time next year we'll be fully in business.

50 BLEACHED

Holy Moly! I have to tell you something outrageous that happened today. I was not there in person, but mom told me the story. I also saw and smelled her when she came home.

Mom had gone to the hardware store to get new filters for our furnace. You know, it's necessary to change them every now and then to have fresh air in the house. Usually this is a quick trip, but this time she took such a long time I feared something had happened. Or maybe she had decided to drop in with her groomer to get highlights? I should definitely have gone with her, should have insisted, but finally I heard the door opening and immediately smelled something was not right.

Mom told me she was in the cashier's line and just about to pay for her stuff when she heard a loud bang, like something crashing on the floor behind her. At the same moment she felt that her shoes and jeans were getting soaked by something much stronger than water. I think water is pretty strong. When you get soaked in it, you get really wet. Anyway, then mom saw an older gentleman behind her and realized he had dropped a gallon of bleach onto the floor. The lid had popped open and the contents had spilled all over the floor - and mom.

How do you react in a situation like that? I have to say I'm proud of myself. I've trained mom not to overreact in sudden, slightly uncomfortable situations. You know, not to scream and yell, not to jump up and down, but calmly assess the damage and carefully evaluate the context in which all this happened. And that's exactly what mom did!

Mom told me that she just got a roll of paper towels from the cashier lady and tried to pat herself dry starting from the jeans. Then she dried her formerly black leather shoes the best she could.

The cashier also provided huge plastic bags so that mom could cover the car seat and the floor mats for her drive back home. This was necessary to prevent a new pattern on her seat upholstery.

Apparently the elderly gentleman was embarrassed. He gave mom a piece of paper with his telephone number so they could get in touch. He said he would like to pay for the damaged goods.

Let me tell you, mom was a sight when she stepped in! Her brown patterned jeans had a creative coloring and a completely new pattern. Some parts were bright white, some kind of golden and others light brown. Her shoes were now dark burgundy and grey.

With the 20/20 hindsight I now have, I was grateful that I didn't need to ride home in the car with mom. I might have gotten white highlights from the smell alone!

Mom got in the shower and changed her clothes. I tried to persuade her to just put the jeans into the washing machine and they'd come out like new, only with a slightly different design, but mom didn't listen. She took a double garbage bag and put her jeans and shoes in there, and threw them away.

Later mom told me she wouldn't call the older man. He had enough embarrassment in the store, and mom said she could afford to buy new shoes and jeans if needed. She had other stuff to wear. I agree with that. I've been in her closet. Many times.

I'm happy it all ended well. Mom's legs were not burned, just thoroughly disinfected, and she still had a faint air of clean around her despite the shower and some perfume.

In hindsight I think it was best mom threw away her bleach-soaked stuff. The smell might not have washed out, and even with the source of the smell gone, I had that strong smell of bleach in my nose for days afterwards.

51 SEARCH AND RESCUE

Yesterday was a feel-good day, but it didn't start that way. Right in the morning there was a lot of commotion and drama with one of our neighbors. You see, there is a mom and a girl in that home, and they have a puppy, a tiny brown Yorkie-Poo. He is the cutest puppy I've seen around here in a long time. His name is Oscar. The girl is about 11, I think, and she always walks him. We've met many times on the sidewalk and in the nearby park. We always sniff each other and exchange nose kisses.

So yesterday morning the girl and Oscar went for a walk in the park. Apparently Oscar was sniffing around in the bushes when the girl got a call on her cellphone. She was talking away and didn't pay that much attention to Oscar. This is my interpretation of course. So when she started to walk again, she got a nasty surprise: Oscar was no longer in his harness! The girl looked around and called him by name, but nothing! She panicked. She was just running towards her house when mom and I were walking towards the park. She was sobbing and told mom that Oscar had escaped from his harness and was nowhere to be found. She didn't understand how that was even possible. I decided I needed to demonstrate to her that it was fairly easy to back out of one's harness. I had done that a couple of times in my youth too, but this was not the time to make her feel even guiltier than she already did. Now was the time for action!

Oscar is so small that the ospreys living in the park may very well see him as a delicious breakfast. There was not one minute to waste. I looked up at the girl who still held Oscar's leash and harness in her hand, and I tried to tell her I wanted to sniff his harness to refresh my memory of his scent. Luckily she got it, and mom too. Mom knows I'm an excellent hunter, like so many generations of poodles before me. There was nothing wrong with my ability to follow a scent, even if my vision was no longer the sharpest. I didn't need to see, I needed to smell, and be able to follow the scent left on the ground and in the air without losing it. I practiced this all the time with the squirrels in our own backyard.

Mom asked the girl to show us the place where Oscar disappeared. She took us to some large shrubs at the end of the wooded area. There I sniffed the harness again and started trailing the scent that had fallen to the ground where Oscar had walked.

I walked carefully with my nose down to the ground and trailed his scent deeper and deeper into the woods. Mom and the girl followed tightly behind me. We came into the grassy area in the middle of the forest where I had found Anna's ring. It was a picnic area with benches, tables, swings and outdoor grills. A family was just getting into their car at the nearby parking lot. Mom and the girl noticed them; I was too busy with my nose on the ground. I followed Oscar's scent to one of the picnic benches, and there it suddenly disappeared. It simply ended right there! What a disappointment! I wanted to help find Oscar and now I had no idea where he had gone. I lifted my head up, put my tail down and looked at mom. That was a sign. She should know that there was no trail to follow from here, and she got it!

Mom and the girl had been looking at the family when they hurriedly got in the car and then sped away. Mom had memorized the tag number, just in case. She thought they seemed in too much of a hurry to get out of there. People normally took their time in the park and drove slowly since the speed limit was a low 15 miles an hour. Something was wrong with this picture. The scent trail disappears, and a car speeds away. We all came to the same conclusion: Oscar had been abducted by that family! He had run into the picnic area and trustingly approached the family. So much for trusting strangers. Oscar was too little to understand that it was dangerous.

Mom took her cellphone and called the police. I heard her telling them how Oscar had run away from his harness, how I had trailed him and then all about the family in the little red car. She gave them the tag number. Of course we could not be absolutely sure that the family was to blame for Oscar's disappearance, but it wouldn't harm anyone if the police checked it out. We had no scent trail to follow in any case so we just walked back to the girl's house to wait for any news from the police officers.

The girl's mom was sad. To my surprise she was not angry with the girl. She thanked me and my mom for the heroic search and rescue effort we had embarked on so swiftly. After only about 25 minutes mom got a call. The police told us they had intercepted the car just after the bridge to the mainland, and they had found Oscar in the car! The family had an explanation of course. They said they saw a puppy run out of the forest, and since he had no collar and no one followed him, they decided to take the puppy to a shelter close to their home. There the staff would be able to check if he had a microchip which would help find his owner. I took that story with a grain of salt, and I think the police did too.

Anyway, the police officers took Oscar away from the family and were now on their way to bring him home. We were so happy! When Oscar came home, the officers praised me for the good work and said I was welcome to help them at any time! When mom told them my name, they asked if I was the same Bumble who had helped the police capture a notorious car thief at the mall some time back. Of course I was. They praised me even more and suggested to mom that she would bring me into the police station the next day so they could give me a small token of appreciation. Mom said she certainly would.

This was my first search and rescue mission. It felt really good to be able to help find little Oscar. He's all grown up now and we see each other regularly in the park. Needless to say he's still grateful for my help.

52 DEPUTY SHERIFF

This morning mom spritzed some strawberry smelling potion all over me. It's supposed to be dry shampoo, make my coat clean and shiny. I don't know about that, but mom believes in its cleaning ability between baths. I'm used to the smell by now. Anyway, she brushed me from top to toe so I would look good when we go to the police station. She cleaned my ears and brushed my teeth. I was representable, as mom put it.

So now we are in her car. She doesn't let me drive today, just because we are going to the Police Station, I guess. It is housed in a large white building in the city center with some other offices. We have to go through a metal detector, just like at the airport. Mom carries me, but needs to put her purse through this little machine where they will look at what's inside. That machine has to have great eyes. I wonder what it thinks about the carrots in mom's purse. It all goes fast and we then walk along a long corridor into the locality where the police officers are housed. I am curious and want to look into the room where the bad guys are held, but mom follows another corridor, and we go into a little reception where we sit down and wait.

After a while a nice looking lady invites us to go into a large office. It says Chief of Police on the door. The Chief is a woman. The police officers I've met have all been men and now their boss is a woman. I think that's neat. She welcomes us and even shakes my paw. She says it's an honor to meet the dog who has assisted her officers two times. I'm trying not to let that go into my head. I want to remain Humble Bumble.

They have set a nice table in the middle of the room with coffee cups, a big cake and dog biscuits for me! We all sit down and enjoy the party. I have my own chair next to moms. She gives me a small piece of the cake, yummy! I get a ton of dog biscuits. Everyone is friendly and soon I feel at home among the officers. If I were younger, I could think of becoming a K9 partner, but I'm happy that I've been able to help out a little bit, even as a laydog.

So after the nice coffee and cake, some other people enter the room. A few of them have cameras, and one has a huge video camera on his shoulder. I think it's a TV guy. Oh my! Now I'm getting a bit nervous. I've never been on TV before.

The Police Chief gives a short speech for me. I sit in my chair, and the cameras are rolling. She praises my wisdom and courage in handling the car thief at the mall and the excellent trailing skills I had demonstrated in search for Oscar. It feels good, I have to admit. Then she hands me a nicely framed white paper. I can't see what's written on it, but it looks official and it has my picture too! Then she fastens a small silver star on the right side of my harness. It is a star for a Sheriff's Deputy. Now I'm excited! I want to jump up and down, but being an educated therapy dog, I curb that impulse. Deputy Sheriff! That's almost like being a real K9 partner. In my mind's eye, I see myself chasing bad characters all over the city.

This is a big day for me and mom too. We're going to watch the local news tonight at 6 p.m. That's when the reportage about my celebration will air, and maybe they will do a short mention again at 10 p.m. I'm looking forward to that, and I feel the weight of responsibility that comes with my new star.

That was a nice event. It's heart-warming that some good deeds are rewarded. When I look back I see how privileged I've been to be able to help out so many times in different, potentially dangerous situations. But I'm still the same Humble Bumble.

53 CANADA NEXT!

I have great news! I just got an invitation to visit my blogging friend Sam. He lives in Canada! I've never been there. I know we have to fly, so I'm taking mom to accompany me. She can have fun with Sam's mom while I'm having fun with Sam. I think that's an excellent deal for both of us.

There is a lot to plan for such a trip, my first one abroad, so I'm trying to get mom going at it right away. First, we need plane tickets. I'm sure there are no direct flights, which is a good thing. I need at least one convenience break, preferably two. I'd better do some ground work right now while mom is at the grocery store.

Ok, here we go. I like to use Expedia because they say "Travel is an Adventure." Travel is so cumbersome nowadays, it should at least be an adventure, right? I know mom doesn't agree. She says adventure in connection with flying is likely to mean delays and canceled flights. And in the worst case scenario there could be an unplanned adventure in an unknown city late at night. With all the trimmings, like trying to find a decent, reasonably priced hotel room for the night instead of sleeping in your own bed or in a friend's house at your destination. She's such a pessimist.

I was right, there are no direct flights from here to Calgary. I can see the shortest flight would be through

Houston, but the layover would be too short even for a potty break. That's not good. There is another flight through Dallas, with an almost two hour layover. That sounds much better. Mom could take me out twice and in between we could eat lunch in a nice restaurant. I could eat mine in the flight bag under the table. I don't mind if the food is delicious, like grilled chicken or something like that. I think I'll leave the page open right here so mom can book the tickets when she comes home. I have to remind her that she needs to check if there is a space left for me on the flights she books. I don't mean the space under the seat in front of her, but I remember that each flight only accepts one or two pets, so mom will need to call the airline to reserve my space too.

I don't need a passport, and mom already has hers, so we're good to go on that front. I do need a health certificate from my doctor though, and he also has to write that I've been vaccinated against rabies. We still have my old certificate somewhere I'm sure, but it says here that it has to be dated within 30 days of travel, so we better see my doctor a few days before the trip. Another reminder to mom. She's lucky to have me to remind her about everything!

Then I have to think about what to bring to Sam. It has to be something durable that he'll have for a long time. I know his mom has cats too so I'll have to plan carefully. Sam says their cats have become quite comfortable lately so it would be cool to help Sam get the cats to do their chores. I wish the Cat Teaser had already been made, but maybe I can build something similar on my own. Hmm, I'll need to build a prototype. Let me get to work immediately while mom is still out. I may need to borrow some of her supplies.

I'm going to mom's walk-in closet. I remember the vest she got last winter. It's not real fur, but it looks real enough. Brown and sleek like a mouse's coat. Yes, there it is! I'm jumping up to get it to fall down from the hanger. Oh, here it comes! Lands right on me, but luckily it's all soft. I get scissors from mom's office and now need to select a suitable piece to suit my purpose. I think I can use one of the two pieces that hang from strings on the front. It would be a pity to cut a piece from the vest itself. Mom might not like it, but I'm sure one hanging piece will be enough for the front. Why would she need two?

Oh, this piece looks like a real mouse! I just have to glue on some black eyes and a tail. I go to fetch the glue from mom's office and then examine mom's sewing basket. Oh here we have it! A roll of black leather string for a tail, and two of the tiniest black buttons for eyes.

While I'm cutting the tail and gluing the eyes on, it becomes a little messy on the carpet in mom's office. I should have gotten a magazine or something as an underlay, but shouldda is too late now. We have a little mess on our hands.

The mouse looks great though. I just need to fasten a string so that Sam can throw it right at the cats from a chair or something, about five feet should do it.

Oh mom, you're home already! I was just making a small present for Sam. I'll clean everything up, I just didn't have the time yet. Oh, I hear a scream from the walk-in closet. Mom comes and gets me. She shows me how she can no longer close the vest. For that she'll need two strings, and now there is only one. Mom looks a bit sad now and that makes me feel bad too. *I'm sorry mom.* My tail goes between my legs. I can't help it.

Mom gets the scissors and cuts out the other string as well. She gives me the other "mouse" too. I'm hoping she'll help me make another present for Sam. She doesn't look too sad. Maybe she can put a new hook closure on the vest. I suggest it, and she finally pets me, a little. Just enough so that I know she has forgiven me.

Making a present for Sam was fun, but I should have planned my project a little better to avoid the mess on the carpet, and maybe I should have asked mom for a small piece of fur to make the mouse. I won't repeat those mistakes. I'm learning.

54 HELLO SAM!

Life is good! We arrived at Sam's house in Canada yesterday afternoon. The trip was long, but the break in Dallas was great. Like I had hoped we had a great meal. Mom had opened my bag a little bit so I could enjoy a few pieces of chicken under the table in the airport restaurant, and I got to go out twice for my business before the second flight.

That flight was boring. What do you do for hours in a flight bag under the seat? I know. You make sure to complete a small but useful chore. Like making a hole at the top of the brand new flight bag. It will enable you to breathe easier, but more importantly to peek out whenever you need to check your surroundings. After three hours of carefully planned and quietly executed biting I saw that the top layer started to thin out, and I saw a little light seep in through the material. That was promising! Then I just nibbled on it a little more and voila, I had my peephole! I could easily have made the hole a bit bigger so that I could have pushed my head through the top to really look out, but I elected not to. It wasn't the right time to make mom angry. But I'm not sure I can resist the temptation on our way back home.

Anyway, Sam's house is nice, warm and homey. Sam is a great friend too. He is a Bishon/Shih Tzu mix with a beautiful white and grey coat and a gorgeous long-haired tail. He's good natured, like me, and he's small like me, even a tiny bit smaller with his full eight pounds. We hit it off right away!

His mom is cool too. She laughs a lot with my mom, and they tell stories about us to each other. I overheard mom telling her about my manufacturing project for the Cat Teaser, which Sam just loved, by the way. Sam's mom said he is a riot! He doesn't look like a riot to me, but I decided to defer judgment until I knew him a bit better.

The only thing I have to get used to is that they have two cats. Pouncer and Notwen. They are cute and seem quite friendly, but I haven't seen those cats chasing mice even once! Sam told me that there is a little conflict brewing between him and the cats. You see, Sam loves boxes. His mom always leaves a box for him in the kitchen, but every time he wants to curl up in his box for a little nap he finds a cat there. Or two! I'm sure they do that just to tease him. Sam asked for my help in attempting to modify that behavior.

A nice opportunity to teach the cats better habits came sooner than we had hoped for. Our moms decided to go out for dinner last night, and Sam's pop was working late. We had the house all to ourselves. As usual, the cats had taken Sam's place in the box his mom had left for him in the kitchen. Now they would get themselves a lesson only two inventive dogs can teach. Sam and I retreated into his mom's bedroom to plan the best approach and to look for supplies we would need for our teach-the-cats-project.

We would dress up as giant rats. That was Sam's idea, and I thought it was nothing short of brilliant. He told me their province was "rat free" so dressing up as rats would teach the cats the best lesson ever! So now we just needed to prepare the costumes and practice the prank. It wouldn't be too difficult. Rats have small heads, big bodies and a long tail. So we checked for suitable materials in all the closets and collected a pile of garments and other essential supplies on the bedroom floor. We closed the door and got to work.

We had found a pair of pants of a brownish woolen material, just like the rats. These pants had wide legs, I think they call it boot cut. We tried them on. Sam crawled into one leg, and I into the other. They fit perfectly! We just needed to cut the legs out and make four holes in each for our legs. That was easy peasy! I'm quite good with measurements and scissors.

In the meantime, Sam went into her mom's bathroom and found some good supplies to tie both ends of the pant legs to our size and to put a hair band loosely around our necks to make an impression of a rat head. We then cut small holes in the "head" for eyes. Almost done, but it was important to make the rats look scary so we looked for something we could use for teeth. We found a pearly white blouse and cut out two pieces for big teeth. We glued them on the face of each costume, slightly below the eye holes, and used a little black marker to separate the teeth so they would look sharp and dangerous. Finally we cut long tails for each costume out of a thin black leather belt and glued them in place. The rats were ready.

We put on the costumes. I almost got scared myself looking at Sam. I asked him to run around in the bedroom to demonstrate our fine design. He truly looked like a huge rat; I've seen one on TV. I'm not kidding! The long tail followed him on the floor when he ran around the bed. This was a successful design project. We were both proud of our creativity and excellent team work. I put on my costume too, and Sam almost fell on his butt. I looked too scary, he said. Then we practiced some rat moves and rat sounds. You know those little squeals. It had to look and feel authentic.

This was my career's best tailoring job. The costumes were terrifying. I knew that, if anything, they would help get the job done. Those cats needed some behavioral adaptation!

55 HELLO CATS!

Now Sam and I were ready for the cats. We sneaked into the kitchen where Pouncer and Notwen were sleeping curled together in Sam's box. They actually looked quite peaceful and cute. One would never know they could be mean to Sam, but as they say, one should not judge a cat by its cover. That goes for dogs too, I guess.

It looked like they were dreaming of tasty dinners. Soon they would realize that giant rats had invaded the house due to their negligence! Sam jumped into position on the top of the box, and I took my position behind the box. We had practiced this and so far everything went according to plan. On the count of three we went into action! Sam started to scratch the top of the box making rat sounds, and I was running wildly around the box with my long tail whooshing past the cats. They were fully alert now wondering what was happening. Next, Sam jumped down and landed right in front of the opening of the box, and I took my position beside him. We squeaked like rats do and showed our improvised black and white teeth. The cats realized they were trapped in the box! They started hissing in sheer desperation. That's what you get when you take over Sam's box! It could become right out dangerous, we squeaked.

We held them in the box for a few seconds, and then ran like lightning behind the wall separating the kitchen and the pantry. We wanted to teach them a simple lesson, not to cause them a heart attack. As soon as the coast was clear, both cats ran out of the box, out of the kitchen and right into the safety of the living room sofa! I've never seen cats sprint that fast!

Sam and I ran back to the bedroom to get rid of our costumes and to clean up a bit. Then we returned to the kitchen. Sam happily took his place in the box, and I went to check on the cats. They were still a bit shaken, but they would be fine. I'm sure we had taught them not to take over Sam's box!

When our moms returned later in the evening, Sam and I kept a low profile. We had tried to clean up in the bedroom best we could by dragging the clothes back into the closet, but the brown pants had now been transformed into nice shorts. I tried to cut the legs more evenly after our showdown with the cats, and hoped Sam's mom didn't mind a new fresh pair of shorts. Warm weather would be here soon enough.

Sam had been right when he said his mom was cool. She saw the pile of clothes and dug out the shorts from underneath the pile. She first looked a bit angry, but when we showed her the costumes we had hid under the bed and explained what we needed the pant legs for, she started smiling. She understood Sam's frustration with the cats. I heard her saying to my mom, "I told you Sam was a riot!" With the benefit of the insights from our little exercise, I think there might be just a hint of truth in it. I guess my mom was not too happy about my creativity with the costumes, but when Sam's mom gave her my costume to take home as a souvenir, she got over her embarrassment and smiled too. Peace in the house. And that included the cats and the dogs.

This morning Sam finally tried out the Cat Teaser. It was funny to watch. As soon as the little mouse appeared in front of the cats, they tried to catch it! I have to praise their vigilance. I think they will leave Sam's box alone for some time to come, and if they go back to their old ways, Sam can always remind them of the giant rats.

For the rest of my visit we took it fairly easy. We were happy to note that the cats had indeed learned their lesson. They never went into Sam's box while I was there, and we saw them actually patrolling the garden for mice. The visit was so much fun! I hope Sam can pay me a visit before too long. And I thought I would never say this, but I would welcome the cats as well. To be completely honest, I got a bit attached to them, and I'm sure there are mice to catch here too.

56 THE LOTTERY

I'm running out of our yard again to see Carmen in the little deli. She gives me a little cookie as usual, but this time I also buy something. A Lotto ticket for tonight's drawing. I had accumulated a small savings of almost 10 dollars, so I thought I should try my luck for one dollar only. Although I don't understand why people think it's so good to have lots and lots of money, I do think a little would be good.

Now it's late in the evening. Mom and dad are sleeping. I go to mom's office and borrow her laptop to check on the winning numbers. *Oh wowff!* If my old eyes don't betray me, all my numbers are the same as the winning ones. I'm a Lotto winner! Can you imagine my good fortune?

I'm sure I'll get more money than I can count, and more than I can haul home in a bag from the deli. Maybe I have to ask mom to take the car so we can pack all the money in the cargo space. I'm sure it'll be big enough. I know there is still plenty of space in our storage room, we can put some boxes of money there too, for the future.

Mom is sleeping so she doesn't know that I've won, not yet. I'll tell her tomorrow. Maybe I'll go to the deli and just take out one small bag first and give it to mom. She'll be so surprised! Usually she only gets love from me and flowers from dad.

I'm hiding the ticket in the cupboard, behind the box where my food cans are. Then I will need to plan what to do with all the money. We have everything we need at home: beds, sofas, tables and chairs, stove, fridge, washer and drier, pots and pans, food and clothes, so we really don't need any more stuff, and if we came up with things we don't need and went to buy them, we would also need to buy a bigger home to house all that stuff we don't need. But that wouldn't make sense, right?

So I'll need to get creative. I know I can use money to help train more dogs. You know, therapy dogs, service dogs for the blind and people with other conditions, emotional support dogs for sick people, K9 partners and I'm sure there are other needs as well, and I would definitely give bags and bags of money to animal shelters. They need more space for homeless animals, and they need more staff. Some shelters need updating too. I would also support foster families so they could take care of more dogs and other animals waiting to find their permanent home.

I could even give scholarships to dogs to go to obedience training if their parents cannot pay the school fees. I could also put up an account in the Smart Pet store for foods for needy pets. Oh, and I could sponsor wellness plans for less privileged dogs in the Pet Hospital, so that they all would get the same care I get when I'm sick.

Then I will need to figure out how to get the money safely to all these different places. A cute looking dog would be an easy target for all kinds of shady figures.

Oh, mom is touching me! "It's time to wake up," she says. I must have dozed off for a moment. That was a strange but wonderful dream, very vivid. I can recall every little detail. The dream could have been an invitation for me to go and see Carmen tonight. It certainly reminded me of the vast need of resources in the common world of animals and people.

I told mom of the dream, and we actually went to buy a ticket from Carmen, but we didn't win. The odds are not that good, mom told me.

She said that to help mobilize money for these good purposes some other action would need to be taken. She mentioned many things we could do, including raising awareness by writing my story. Thanks mom for this excellent idea. I'm doing it right now!

57 TOMORROW

Tomorrow is Sunday and my 13th birthday! In people years, for a small breed like mine, it means that I would be somewhere close to 70 years old! *Whoaa.* I'm actually much older than mom and dad. I have to remind them about that once the birthday celebrations are over. Respect your elders, and give them some additional privileges. They are doing pretty good, but a gentle reminder is always in place.

Some people may think I should be considering retirement, but I don't think so. My volunteer work with old people in the Evening Sun and with kids at the Children's Hospital is so rewarding. I've decided to be a therapy dog for many more moons to come. As for my day job, protecting our home, I think I'm still doing it pretty well. I have the best hearing and a young man's bark. Even if my eyesight is not at its absolute best anymore, it doesn't really matter. One can't see from the outside who is a good and who is a bad person. The good or the bad is all inside. I've learned to understand that in my time. I can actually sense the good and the bad. Did you know that a person emits invisible energy? It's like a tiny vibration in the air. A bad person has a vibe of anger or fear and a good person has a vibe of love or kindness. These vibes are very different. I learned to distinguish them already when I was growing up.

I have to tell you one more true story. One day when I was still living in my first house, a nicely attired, handsome man knocked on the door. When the woman opened the door, he asked if he could use the phone. He said his car broke down, and his cellphone's battery was dead. Immediately I sensed a negative vibe of fear and agitation. Not a good man. So I started barking. When the woman told me to be quiet, I stopped barking but took on a low growl instead from deep inside my breast. I knew he was lying. He was up to no good.

When the woman went into the kitchen to get the cordless phone, I stood in front of the door that was left slightly ajar. I growled louder and even showed my teeth. I was telling the man that if he tries to come into the house, I would be quick to bite him. Hard. So he stayed on the front steps and waited for the phone. When the woman came back with the phone, she again told me to be quiet and not to disturb the nice man.

Then he dialed a number, walked a few steps down the driveway, turned his back to the house and spoke very quickly, much like the people who live in New York. Then he gave the phone back to the woman, walked down the street and disappeared from sight. I told the woman I had to go out to do my business. It wasn't a lie because I really had to, but I also wanted to run down to the sidewalk and see his broken down car. There was no car and no man in sight. Something was badly wrong. I just knew it.

In the evening the woman opened the TV to watch the 6 o'clock news. I was resting under the living room sofa table and the news caught my attention too. The anchor woman said that a dangerous man had escaped from the county jail early in the morning. He was the main suspect in a robbery that had taken place around lunch time at the men's clothing store. Nice clothes and money were taken. The store's owner was found in the storage room with his hands and feet bound with a thick rope. Luckily he was unharmed. They also showed a photo of a man in a jail bird outfit. His appearance was different, but I knew it was the same man who had come to the house in the afternoon. I heard the woman scream and then go to the phone. She called the police and told them the escaped prisoner had come to the house.

She didn't say anything to me. Not the slightest recognition that I was right about the man. It didn't matter because she never gave me recognition anyway, but I hope she learned that one cannot judge a person based on how they look, how they speak or what kind of clothes they wear.

I've told you about many of my experiences and adventures. I've had my trials, but many more good days. I'm not living in the past. I just appreciate that I've seen a lot of life and learned tons of things. I've become wiser from it. The present day is always a gift given to me, but I have to confess that today I can't help but live a little bit in the future too. Tomorrow is February 2, 2014, my 13th birthday. It's also the big Game Day. Super Bowl. I hope mom and dad get their priorities right. I'm expecting an exciting day! Surprises and treats. Maybe we'll go skydiving or something equally invigorating.

And we'll go for walks, we'll exercise, we'll eat and have fun! Me and my family. Whatever is in store for me tomorrow, and for the rest of my life for that matter, you should know that I'll enjoy every minute of it! I hope you will too.

ABOUT THE AUTHOR

Helen Kuusela spent her early years in Finland and Sweden where she earned her Bachelors and Masters degrees in management. She then embarked on a career in international development which took her and her family to numerous countries on several continents. In mid-1990's she settled in the US and now lives with her family in Florida, where she also runs an international consulting practice.

She is a passionate owner of a sweet rescue dog and a regular contributor to animal rescue organizations. She has committed to donate a part of the proceeds from this book to the local Humane Society shelter in the county where she lives.

Over her successful career, Helen has written numerous professional publications focusing on people and organizational management. She is also an avid writer and poet in the blogging world and is preparing to publish her first poetry collection and another novel later in 2014.

www.ingramcontent.com/pod-product-compliance
Lightning Source LLC
Chambersburg PA
CBHW061943070426
42450CB00007BA/1032